Canada in the Atlantic Economy

CANADA IN THE ATLANTIC ECONOMY

Published:

Forthcoming:

Trade Liberalization
and the Canadian Steel Industry

Jacques Singer

Published for the
Private Planning Association of Canada by University of Toronto Press

To William B. Lambert

These studies of "Canada in the Atlantic Economy" are dedicated with respect and gratitude to the late William B. Lambert, Chairman of the Board of the Private Planning Association of Canada from 1965 to 1967, who played a vital role in the development and supervision of the Atlantic Economic Studies Program, on which the publications are based.

His interest went far beyond his formal responsibility; he held a deep conviction concerning the importance of international cooperation among the North Atlantic nations. His untimely death came when the first draft studies had entered the early stages of publication.

© University of Toronto Press 1969 / Printed in Canada / SBN 8020 3230 3

Foreword

There have been two outstanding developments in international trade policy during the past twenty years—the multilateral dismantling of trade barriers under the General Agreement on Tariffs and Trade, which has been the agency for several rounds of successful tariff negotiations since its inception in 1947, and the establishment of the European Economic Community and the European Free Trade Association in the late 1950s. In a period of reconstruction and then sustained growth, these policies have helped the participating nations of the Atlantic area to experience the benefits of international specialization and expanding trade. The wealth generated by trade and domestic prosperity has also made possible external aid programs to assist economic growth in the developing countries.

Whatever the trade and economic development problems of the future, it is widely acknowledged that the industrially advanced countries of the North Atlantic region must play an important role. It is also generally conceded that the ability of these countries to maintain their own economic growth and prosperity and to contribute to that of the less advanced nations will be greatly enhanced if they can reduce or remove the remaining trade barriers among themselves. Cooperation among Atlantic countries is now fostered by the GATT and by the Organisation for Economic Co-operation and Development. But the success of these and other approaches depends on the assessment by each country of the importance of international trade liberalization and policy coordination for its domestic economy and other national interests. This is particularly true for countries such as Canada which are heavily dependent upon export markets.

The Atlantic Economic Studies Program of the Private Planning Association of Canada was initiated to study the implications for Canada of trade liberalization and closer economic integration among the nations bordering the North Atlantic. It is planned to issue at least twelve paperbound volumes, incorporating over twenty studies by leading Canadian and foreign economists. Despite the technical nature of much of the subject matter, the studies have been written in language designed to appeal to the non-professional reader.

The directors and staff of the Private Planning Association wish to acknowledge the financial support which made this project possible—a grant from the Ford Foundation and the contributions of members of the Association. They are also appreciative of the help that has been provided by very many individuals in the preparation and review of all the studies— in discussions and correspondence with authors, at the Association's November, 1966, conference on "Canada and the Atlantic Economy," and on other occasions.

H. E. ENGLISH
Director of Research
Atlantic Economic Studies Program

Acknowledgment

The author gratefully acknowledges the permission given by The Algoma Steel Corporation, Limited, to use statistical exhibits published in the company's submission, to the Minister of Finance, on the report of the Royal Commission on Taxation (August, 1967).

Abbreviations

AISI	American Iron and Steel Institute
BLEU	Belgium-Luxembourg Economic Union
BLS	Bureau of Labor Statistics
BOF	Basic oxygen furnace
ECE	Economic Commission for Europe
ECSC	European Coal and Steel Community
EFTA	European Free Trade Association
NBER	National Bureau of Economic Research
OECD	Organisation for Economic Co-operation and Development
OEEC	Organisation for European Economic Co-operation
VÖEST	Vereinigte Österreichische Eisen und Stahlwerke, A.G.

Contents

Introduction

This study analyzes the competitive position of the Canadian primary iron
and steel industry among major steel industries of the Atlantic nations—
those of the United States, the European Coal and Steel Community (ECSC),
the United Kingdom, the six other European Free Trade Area (EFTA)
nations, and Japan. The terms of reference for this project (established under
the Atlantic Economic Studies Program of the Private Planning Association
of Canada), require analysis of the prospects for, and impacts of, alternative
arrangements for freer trade in steel products among Canada and other
Atlantic nations. Thus this project had to be elastic in its approach, accommodating not only the major events influencing the conduct of world steel
trade that have recently taken place, but also developments with important
implications whose final outcome is still uncertain. For example, since the
inception of the project, the Kennedy round negotiations have been completed, and it is clear that the important impact on the Canadian steel industry
will not be tariff changes but rather the new international anti-dumping agreement, which requires new Canadian legislation changing the existing automatic anti-dumping provisions.

While the Kennedy round conference pursued its lengthy negotiations,
world steel markets felt the growing competitive pressure of excess capacity
in steel-producing facilities among the world's major steel producers. This
explains the growing pressure exercised by U.S. steel-industry interests on
the U.S. Congress to deal with the "steel import problem." Similarly, excess
capacity and its influence on world steel trade constituted the major catalyst
bringing about the first annual conference of the International Iron and
Steel Institute at Brussels in November, 1967.

Other events which this study has had to take into account, even though
their implications are by no means capable of formulation into final conclusions, include the recent renationalization of steel in Great Britain, now
joined by devaluation of the pound, and a number of important developments
among the ECSC group, including steps taken by individual national governments in support of their industries.

Since the draft of this study was completed, a number of major events have taken place in the world steel picture which have significant implications for this analysis. These include the cracks that appeared in the U.S. steel-price structure late in 1968 and, more significantly in early 1969, the agreement on voluntary cutbacks in steel exports from Japan and the ECSC countries into the United States. Unfortunately, it was not possible to weave the implications of these developments into the mainstream of this study.

The organization of this study emphasizes international trade. The descriptive material in chapter 1 on the Canadian primary iron and steel industry is held to the minimum required to update earlier, more comprehensive studies,[1] and it provides a summary view of the structure and the performance of the industry during the postwar period and particularly during the last decade.

Chapter 2 shifts to matters of more direct concern under the terms of reference of the Atlantic Economic Studies Program (AESP); its objective is to provide a survey of steel-trading trends in order to define the "moods" and reactions one would expect from various nations' steel industries to proposals designed to liberalize steel trade. The chapter deals with the global steel-trading picture, with special emphasis on those nations to which the "Atlantic" reference appears to be specifically applicable with respect to steel. Although the study does not provide a detailed analysis of the steel industry of each of these countries, it sketches the setting of the steel industries in the United States, the member countries of the ECSC, the United Kingdom (and other EFTA countries), and finally—because of its rapidly growing importance in the international steel community—Japan. Chapter 2 concludes with an analysis of Canadian steel-trade trends.

Chapter 3, the final chapter of this study, deals with the subject of private and public commercial policy in international trade, then draws conclusions under the terms of reference of the study. More specifically, the chapter begins with an analysis of offshore steel-pricing policies, proceeds into the question of dumping and the new international anti-dumping agreement, summarizes the steel tariffs of Canada and other major steel-producing countries, makes an analysis of non-tariff commercial-policy factors, and concludes with an evaluation of the prospects and impacts of freer international trade in steel among the Atlantic nations.

[1]See, for example, *The Canadian Primary Iron and Steel Industry* (prepared for the Royal Commission on Canada's Economic Prospects by the Bank of Nova Scotia), Oct. 1956; and Tariff Board, *Basic Iron and Steel Products, Reference 118*, Ottawa, 1957.

1. The Structure and Performance of the Canadian Primary Iron and Steel Industry: A Post-World War II Perspective

Introduction and historical summary

The Canadian primary iron and steel industry scores high both by the standards of performance of the Canadian economy and by the tests one can devise for comparing industries across international boundaries. It is an industry that has surged ahead, from its modest beginnings as a small, tariff-protected industry, to become a reasonably large giant (ranking tenth in world output of raw steel in 1966) able for the most part, as this study suggests, to stand on its own feet internationally.

The beginnings of the iron and steel industry date back to the period following the National Policy of 1879, which was designed partly to foster a Canadian steel industry. The forerunners of three of today's "Big Four"[1]— Stelco at Hamilton, Algoma at Sault Ste. Marie, Ontario, and Dosco at Sydney, Nova Scotia—were established in the decade 1895–1905; and from a level of output of less than 100,000 tons of pig iron and only 26,000 tons of steel in 1900, the fledgling industry launched into an initial takeoff that was to carry output to more than 1.1 million tons of both pig iron and steel in 1913. Except for the larger requirements of World War I, this was to be the peak production year until 1928 and 1929, as the rolling mill facilities of the Canadian steel industry were not adapted to the new demand trends appearing in the 1920s, particularly in the construction and the automotive industries. The peacetime production peak of 1929 gave way to an abysmal decline in the depressed 1930s; only in 1937 and 1939 did output manage to match the previous 1929 peak.

World War II and the postwar period mark a new phase in the development of the Canadian steel industry. From a capacity of approximately 2.2 million tons of raw steel on the eve of World War II, the production facilities of the industry were expanded to some 3.2 million tons by the end of the war.

[1]The "Big Four" companies are The Steel Company of Canada Limited (Stelco), The Algoma Steel Corporation, Limited (Algoma), Dominion Foundries and Steel Limited (Dofasco), and Dominion Steel and Coal Corporation Limited (Dosco). Early in 1968, Dosco's Sydney, Nova Scotia, mill was taken over by the province of Nova Scotia and now operates as Sydney Steel Corporation.

Following an initial round of peacetime expansion to a level of 3.7 million tons in the early 1950s, large increases in investment expenditures in the fifteen years since 1954 brought raw steel capacity over the 5-million-ton mark in 1956, above 10 million tons in 1965, and on to 11.7 million tons in 1967. As Table 1 shows, the utilization of this raw steel capacity remained relatively high until 1965 (except in recession years).

TABLE 1

STEEL-FURNACE CAPACITY, CANADA, AT JANUARY 1, 1946–67
(volume figures in thousands of net tons)

	Raw steel capacity				Production of raw steel as a percentage of raw steel capacity
	Basic open-hearth	Electric	Oxygen	Total raw steel capacity	
1946	2,745	461		3,206	72.6
1947	2,745	471		3,216	91.6
1948	2,750	464		3,214	99.6
1949	3,024	528		3,552	89.8
1950	3,024	667		3,691	91.7
1951	2,949	682		3,631	98.3
1952	2,949	729		3,678	100.7
1953	3,757	714		4,472	90.0
1954	3,919	738		4,657	66.9
1955	3,813	720	350	4,883	91.1
1956	4,078	769	350	5,197	99.7
1957	4,270	675	525	5,470	90.2
1958	4,497	706	710	5,913	72.1
1959	4,521	707	1,086	6,314	91.8
1960	4,477	700	1,440	6,617	86.3
1961	4,477	1,021	1,580	7,078	90.1
1962	5,045	969	1,870	7,884	89.4
1963	5,045	931	2,100	8,076	99.9
1964	5,420	1,016	2,550	8,986	99.8
1965	5,921	1,325	3,100	10,345	95.4
1966	6,270	1,435	3,550	11,255	87.2
1967	6,470	1,617	3,630	11,717	81.6

Sources: Dominion Bureau of Statistics, *Primary Iron and Steel*, cat. no. 41-001, 1964 to 1967, and *Iron and Steel Mills*, cat. no. 41-203, for 1946 to 1963.

The expansion path of the Canadian primary iron and steel industry in the postwar period can be thought of as having taken place in the form of parallel (though by no means always completely balanced) growth in pig iron, raw steel, and rolling-mill-product facilities—with the rate of growth and mix of demand for various types of rolling mill products dictating the speed of the full expansion of the vertically integrated structure. (In addition, the companies in the industry have also made large investment commitments for the provision of raw materials and fabricating operations.)

Our statistical emphasis in this study is on steel in its finished form as far as the primary iron and steel industry is concerned. These are mostly rolling mill products,[2] and it is both the expansion of rolling mill facilities and the construction of mills to produce new products for the rapidly rising amount of steel required by Canadian users (thus reducing Canada's dependence on imported steel) that can be thought of as having provided the impetus for the large increases in raw material supplies and production facilities for other stages of the steel-manufacturing process. One further reason for our emphasis on rolling mill products is that most of the world's steel trade takes place in rolling-mill-product form, with relatively little pig iron, ingot, or semi-finished steel crossing international boundaries.

As a result of the industry's growth in Canada, domestic users of rolled steel, who depended on foreign sources of supply for almost two-thirds of their requirements after World War I and one-third after World War II, could look to domestic sources of supply for some 90 percent of their needs by the early 1960s. The building of new facilities since then—particularly for rolling wide plate and heavy structurals—has raised the degree of domestic self-sufficiency even further. At present, the only gap in the Canadian industry's rolling mill facilities is in heavy structurals exceeding a 24-inch width. However, Canadian mills may not roll as wide a selection of widths and lengths of various products as their U.S. or overseas competitors (even though theoretically they have the capacity) because orders for them are in smaller quantities than are required for minimum-scale economic production runs.

Industry structure and postwar performance

A. BASIC STRUCTURAL CHARACTERISTICS

The Canadian primary iron and steel industry is dominated by four large, integrated producers whose operations span from the production of coke, on to pig iron and steel ingots, and further into a diversity of rolling mill products sold to final users. In addition, these producers are integrated to various degrees "backward" into mining operations, thereby providing a substantial portion of their iron ore and, in some cases, coking coal requirements, and in some instances "forward" into further fabrication operations. To these companies—The Algoma Steel Corporation, Limited, Dosco Steel Limited,

[2]Some pig iron and ingot is sold for export and for use in other industries; similarly some semi-finished steel bypasses the rolling operation of the industry for use elsewhere.

Dominion Foundries and Steel Limited, and The Steel Company of Canada Limited—the term integrated is usually applied.

Figure 1 shows the location of the industry's production facilities. The largest concentration of facilities is on the Niagara Peninsula, where the facilities of Stelco and Dofasco make Hamilton, Ontario, Canada's leading steel-production centre; smaller plants in the area include Atlas Steels' plant at Welland, Burlington Steel, also at Hamilton, and Lake Ontario Steel at Whitby.[3]

The production facilities of Algoma Steel are mainly based at Sault Ste. Marie, Ontario, and are, by comparison with those of Stelco and Dofasco, relatively far from the heavily concentrated steel markets in southern Ontario. This locational disadvantage, however, is offset by Algoma's proximity to iron ore deposits, which thus partly compensates for outgoing-freight cost disadvantages by lower raw material assembly costs. Historically, Algoma became the first among the Ontario-based producers to integrate backward towards iron ore operations.

The rolling mill facilities of the large Ontario producers closely reflect the demand requirements of the durable-goods industries and the construction markets of southern Ontario. Dofasco, for example, has concentrated all its rolling facilities in the flat-rolled product groups, and particularly in the production of cold-rolled strip and sheet and tin-plate. Stelco's rolling facilities extend virtually across the entire line of rolling mill products, with the major exception of heavy structurals and rails. Algoma's growth pattern in the last fifteen years resulted in a significant expansion of flat-rolled and heavy structural rolling facilities (including wide flange beams) which reduced the company's relatively high dependence on rail, bar, light structural, and semi-finished steel sales that existed previously. Its large investment into the rolling of heavy structurals, a product group which had been supplied mainly by imports, was a significant factor in reducing one of the remaining gaps in the product structure of Canadian producers.

The operations of the main plant of Dosco at Sydney, Nova Scotia, were taken over by the province of Nova Scotia early in 1968. The mill has pig iron and ingot facilities, integrated with blooming and billet facilities, a rod and bar mill, and a rail mill. As Dosco's rolling and fabricating facilities are located at the Montreal works and the Contrecoeur works in Quebec, the company was in a position of having to supply "raw materials" for these mills over a considerable distance.[4] Additional production facilities in the

[3]These three companies are not integrated into pig iron production and produce their ingot requirements in electric furnaces.
[4]The Montreal works has a steel ingot capacity of only 156,000 tons.

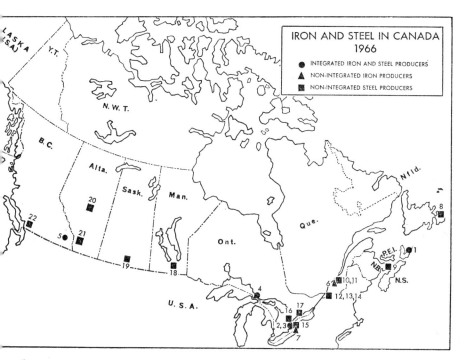

ıure 1
ırce: Department of Energy, Mines and Resources, *Primary Iron and Steel*, Jan. 1967, Operators
∟ist, Part 1.

Montreal area include Atlas' stainless steel mill at Tracy[5] and Stelco's mill at Contrecoeur.[6]

The western portion of the industry consists of a number of relatively small plants, using scrap metal as a raw material and producing steel mostly in electric furnaces. In the Prairie provinces the largest are the Manitoba Rolling Mill Division of Dominion Bridge Company in Winnipeg, Manitoba; Interprovincial Steel and Pipe at Regina, Saskatchewan; and Stelco's Premier works at Edmonton, Alberta. In British Columbia, the main production facilities are the plants of the Consolidated Mining and Smelting Company at Kimberley[7] and its melting and rolling plant at Western Canada Steel in Vancouver. The rolling mill products of these western plants reflect mainly the composition of regional demand—merchant bars, reinforcing bars, light structurals, rods, and, in the case of Interprovincial Steel and Pipe, plate, skelp, and hot-rolled sheets and coils.

B. SIZE, CONCENTRATION, AND OWNERSHIP

In 1967 the "Big Four" of the industry accounted for 93.4 percent of total pig iron capacity and 85.3 percent of its raw steel capacity. The fifth major steel company, Atlas Steels, produces its steel in electric furnaces at Welland, Ontario, and Tracy, Quebec, and is Canada's leading stainless steel specialty producer.

The degree of concentration among the four largest companies in the industry is also relatively high. Stelco, the largest company, accounted for almost 36 percent of the industry's total raw steel capacity in 1967. It is followed by Algoma with 21 percent, and Dofasco, 18 percent. Dosco, with 10 percent of the total, was the smallest among the four. At the time of this study Dosco's Sydney, Nova Scotia, plant has been taken over by the province of Nova Scotia.[8]

The industry has a relatively high degree of domestic ownership and control. At the end of 1963, 80 percent of the capital employed was owned in Canada, and 86 percent of the capital employed was controlled in Canada. These ratios are exceeded among manufacturing industries only by those of beverages and textiles. Among individual companies, one of the Big Four (Dosco) is foreign (U.K.) controlled. Also a large, but non-controlling, block of the common shares of The Algoma Steel Corporation, Limited is

[5]The Atlas mill has a capacity of 70,000 tons of crude stainless steel, a continuous-casting machine, and a stainless sheet and strip mill.
[6]The Stelco mill produces pipe and hollow structural tubing, merchant bar, reinforcing bar, and light structural shapes.
[7]Cominco is now integrated into pig iron production at Kimberley.
[8]The change leaves Dosco with two electric arc furnaces at the Montreal works for its steel supply.

held by the German Mannesmann group. An interesting phenomenon is the virtual absence of U.S.-controlled companies in this industry; the only exception of any consequence is a specialty stainless steel producer in Quebec, The Crucible Steel Company of Canada Limited, which is a subsidiary of a parent company of a similar name in the United States.

This relatively high degree of domestic control and ownership of the steel industry is characteristic of every major steel industry in the world. In the reconstruction and rapid growth of the steel industry around the world in the postwar period, international boundary lines have scarcely been crossed.[9]

C. OUTPUT AND DEMAND TRENDS

A number of alternatives are open for measuring output and demand of the primary iron and steel industry, as the integrated production processes involve successive conversion of raw materials (iron ore, coke, and limestone) into pig iron; pig iron (and/or scrap) into ingots (raw steel); and the rolling of ingots into a variety of rolling mill products. Since relatively little pig iron or ingot steel is sold as final products, the bulk of the marketable output of the industry consists of rolling mill products (a classification of these is shown in Table 3).

All the statistics describing the steel-production process point to a picture of rapid growth in the postwar period. Detailed output statistics for pig iron, raw steel, and rolling mill products are shown in Tables 2 and 3. Pig iron production amounted to 1.4 million tons in the first peacetime year (1946) and averaged 2.1 million tons between 1947 and 1949. It reached the 3-million-ton level in 1953, 4.2 million tons in 1959, and exceeded 7 million tons in both 1965 and 1966. For the years 1946 to 1966, pig iron production shows an annual compound rate of growth of 8.5 percent; this is somewhat larger than rate-of-growth computations for raw steel and rolling mill products, partly because a rather large volume of pig iron exports has been built up during the postwar period (tonnages were nominal after the war and have ranged between 500,000 and 600,000 tons annually in recent years).[10]

Raw steel output, amounting to 2.3 million tons in 1946 and averaging 3.1 million tons in the years 1947 to 1949, rose to 5.3 million tons in 1956,

[9]Interestingly, American entrepreneurs were instrumental in establishing the predecessor companies of both Stelco and Algoma. Department of Energy, Mines and Resources, *Mineral Information Bulletin*, MR70, pp. 7 and 8. In addition, a Boston financier provided capital for Dosco, and C. W. Sherman came from the United States with his capital to found Dofasco.

[10]Scrap is the other raw material used in the steel-making process, and the mix used between scrap and pig iron depends partly upon relative prices. Typical scrap ratios are 50 percent for open-hearth furnaces, 30 percent for basic oxygen furnaces, and 99 percent for electric furnaces.

TABLE 2

PRODUCTION OF PIG IRON AND
RAW STEEL,[a] CANADA, 1946–67
(thousands of net tons)

	Pig iron	Raw steel[a]
1946	1,406	2,327
1947	1,963	2,946
1948	2,126	3,200
1949	2,154	3,190
1950	2,317	3,384
1951	2,553	3,569
1952	2,682	3,703
1953	3,012	4,116
1954	2,211	3,195
1955	3,215	4,535
1956	3,568	5,302
1957	3,718	5,038
1958	3,060	4,345
1959	4,183	5,900
1960	4,299	5,809
1961	4,926	6,467
1962	5,289	7,174
1963	5,915	8,190
1964	6,541	9,131
1965	7,065	10,029
1966	7,213	10,003
1967	6,940	9,694

Source: DBS, *Primary Iron and Steel*,
cat. no. 41-001.
[a]Raw steel and castings.

7.2 million tons in 1962, and exceeded the 10-million-ton mark in 1965 and 1966. This amounts to an annual growth rate between 1946 and 1966 of 7.6 percent.

Total Canadian shipments of rolling mill products were 1.9 million tons in 1946; by 1956 they exceeded the 4-million-ton level; and in 1965 and 1966 they amounted to 7.1 million tons. Here the implied annual rate of growth between 1946 and 1966 is 6.8 percent.

The primary iron and steel component of the DBS Index of Industrial Production[11] shows an annual growth rate of 6.9 percent in the period 1946 to 1966, inclusive.[12] As the more detailed statistics in Table 3 show, output

[11]The index is based on the weighted net output of (1) production of ferro-alloys and production for sale of pig iron and steel ingots, (2) carbon steel castings and alloy steel castings, and (3) production (net, less producers' interchange) of eighteen individual types of rolling mill products. DBS, *Revised Index of Industrial Production 1935–1957, Reference Paper*, cat. no. 61-502, 1959, p. 57.
[12]Based on a least-squares, logarithmic trend.

TABLE 3

MILL SHIPMENTS OF ROLLING MILL PRODUCTS, CANADA, 1955–67
(thousands of tons)

	1955	1956	1957	1958	1959	1960	1961	1962	1963	1964	1965	1966	1967
Total rolling mill products	3,459	4,053	3,840	3,361	4,458	4,338	4,604	5,123	5,917	6,710	7,102	7,129	6,945
1. Semi-finished steel shapes	290	84	158	171	242	443	308	313	307	378	383	326	336
2. Heavy structural steel shapes	173	250	265	146	182	167	236	358	378	462	442	433	374
3. Rails	215	360	400	360	286	226	194	231	339	269	214	282	279
4 Track material	94	119	110	83	99	55	60	77	79	81	56	63	57
5. Bars:	731	908	850	706	905	828	906	988	1,119	1,342	1,497	1,507	1,389
Bar-sized structural shapes	77	78	77	69	75	65	75	82	91	106	100	87	124
Concrete-reinforcing bars	217	295	284	281	321	348	404	394	426	564	643	656	495
Other hot-rolled bars	392	484	451	321	463	377	388	465	544	603	680	686	695
Cold-rolled bars	45	46	37	35	46	37	38	48	58	69	75	79	75
6. Wire rods	359	399	294	268	378	346	356	352	392	442	445	428	425
7. Flat hot-rolled products:	784	957	1,019	827	1,200	1,161	1,342	1,429	1,736	1,885	2,083	2,093	2,111
Plate (excluding for pipe)	285	329	349	229	414	372	404	484	546	619	735	712	576
Hot-rolled sheet and strip (excluding for pipe)	254	281	303	257	450	459	435	595	737	755	825	863	910
Skelp	244	347	366	341	336	330	503	351	453	512	524	518	625
8. Flat cold-rolled products:	813	977	745	800	1,165	1,112	1,201	1,374	1,568	1,850	1,982	1,995	1,974
Cold-rolled and coated sheet and strip (excluding galvanized)	654	770	571	603	859	831	863	1,009	1,180	1,375	1,462	1,454	1,438
Galvanized sheet	159	207	174	197	306	281	337	365	388	475	520	541	536

Source: Submission by The Algoma Steel Corporation, Limited, to the Minister of Finance, on the Report of the Royal Commission on Taxation, Statistical Supplement, Aug. 1967, Tables 10.1 to 10.9.2 (hereafter referred to as the Algoma Supplement), from 1955 to 1966. Figures for 1967 compiled from DBS, *Primary Iron and Steel*, Dec. 1967.

Note: Details may not add to totals because of rounding.

trends among individual rolling mill products differ materially, depending upon the fortunes of various sectors and industries where they are used. For example, the demand for rails and track materials shows a downward trend, while the market for skelp (which is further processed into line pipe) and galvanized sheets (widely used in consumer durables and construction) has grown very rapidly.

The sharp rise in Canadian steel output during the postwar period can be traced to a number of reinforcing factors:

1. A relatively rapid over-all growth in the economy, accompanied by a magnified expansion of demand from the important steel-using industries and sectors of the economy: construction, consumer durable-goods industries, and machinery and equipment industries.[13]

2. A general trend towards increasingly larger participation by Canadian-based manufacturing operations in the consumer durable-goods industries, which has been further reinforced in recent years by the U.S.-Canadian automotive products agreement. In terms of the market for rolled steel, this may be thought of as having provided a potential for "indirect" import substitution.

3. The direct substitution of steel imports through the enlargement of existing production facilities and the building of new ones.

Although Canada still remains one of the smaller members on the international steel ladder, the realization of the opportunities opened to the industry resulted not only in a high growth rate in the industry's output relative to over-all economic growth in the postwar period, but also in a respectable performance by international standards. (Tables 4 and 5.)

As one would expect in a durable-goods industry supplying a number of highly cyclical sectors and manufacturing industries, the longer-term growth in the output of steel has not been smooth or without interruption. The business recessions of the postwar period—1953 to 1954, 1957 to 1958, and 1960 to 1961—each had a short, though relatively sharp, impact on the industry's output. Figure 2 shows the index of industrial production for primary iron and steel, in seasonally adjusted form, for the entire postwar period. Peaks and troughs in output, separating periods of expansion and recession, are given in Table 6. The annual data for ingot production and rolling mill shipments shown in Tables 2 and 3 somewhat understate these cyclical patterns, but here also there is evidence of the impact of recession.[14]

The strategy of the industry under the conditions of general prosperity and

[13]Because imports still provide a large part of Canadian machinery requirements, the relative importance of the last group for Canadian steel demand is smaller than in other countries (e.g., the United States, the United Kingdom, and West Germany).
[14]The 1958 results on a yearly basis are distorted by an August to November strike which interrupted the output of one of the large companies.

13 CANADIAN IRON AND STEEL INDUSTRY

TABLE 4

INTERNATIONAL COMPARISONS OF ANNUAL PERCENTAGE
INCREASES IN STEEL PRODUCTION, 1950–66

	Raw steel output (millions of net tons)		Average annual increase (percentages)
	1950	1966	
United States	96.8	134.1	2.0
Canada	3.4	10.0	7.0
Japan	5.3	52.7	15.4
ECSC	35.0	93.8	6.3
United Kingdom	18.2	27.2	2.5

Source: U.S. Senate, Committee on Finance, *Steel Import Study*, Washington, 1967 (hereafter cited as *Steel Import Study*), Table A-6, pp. 256–61.

TABLE 5

COMPARATIVE GROWTH RATES, SELECTED SECTORS AND
INDUSTRIES, CANADA, 1946–66
(percentages)

	Growth rate 1946–66
Real domestic product	4.48
Real domestic product, less agriculture	4.79
Index of industrial production:	5.70
Manufacturing	4.90
Durable manufactures	4.91
Iron and steel products	4.96
Primary iron and steel	6.89

Note: Growth rates are least-squares of logarithms.
Source: DBS, *Index of Industrial Production*, cat. no. 61-005, June 1967.

a rapidly growing demand for steel appears to have been made up of the following elements:
1. The rapid adaptation of new technology, which, as we note below, may have been, on balance, encouraging to a scale of operations suitable for the size of the Canadian market.
2. The opportunities to enlarge and fill out its product structure by economically scaled production runs, thus achieving a relatively high ratio of capacity utilization, efficiency, and profitability. This approach left to imports the dual role of providing those products for which the Canadian market was insufficient in size to permit efficient production runs and of supplying "peak" cyclical demand, when the requirements of heavy investment programs would

Figure 2 Index of Industrial Production, Primary Iron and Steel (seasonally adjusted, 1949 = 100).
Source: DBS, *Index of Industrial Production*, cat. no. 61-005.

TABLE 6

INDEX OF INDUSTRIAL PRODUCTION,
PRIMARY IRON AND STEEL
(seasonally adjusted, 1949 = 100)

Peak		Trough	
March, 1953	141.0	May, 1954	103.5
August, 1956	197.0	May, 1958	145.5
December, 1959	231.2	July, 1960	165.6
March, 1966	346.0	August, 1967[a]	297.2

[a]Rather than Jan. 1967 which is irregularly low because of a strike against one mill.

have called for an amount of production capacity that would have proven excessive in relation to longer-term growth requirements.

3. The gradual adoption of definite price policy, making Canadian steel attractive relative to U.S. imports (which had historically been the major source of external supply).

Several distinguishing characteristics arise out of the postwar performance of the Canadian steel industry that have an important bearing on our subsequent international trade analysis:

1. As already noted in the introductory sketch, the ratio of domestic steel supply to apparent consumption of steel in Canada has risen over the long run. Data compiled by the Tariff Board show that this ratio amounted to more than 35 percent in 1922, 45 percent in 1929, and 61 percent in 1937. At the beginning of the post-World War II period, this ratio had risen to 70 percent in 1946 and 72 percent in 1948. From then on there were further small gains, leading to a position where domestic sources provided approximately three-quarters of all steel requirements in the years 1953 to 1956.

The annual data in terms of rolling mill products (see Table 47) show that in response to the major capital investment boom of the mid-1950s, there was a cyclical upsurge in steel imports. In both 1956 and 1957, the ratio of imports to apparent consumption was thus close to 30 percent. Following this, the impact of the 1957–58 recession on steel demand and a sharp expansion in the productive capacity of the industry take over. Sharp declines in the relative importance of imports continued until 1962 and 1963, when the ratio of imports to total apparent consumption averaged only 13 percent. Following this, a cyclical upsurge in imports appears again in response to the new boom of capital expenditures. Imports in 1964 and 1965 accounted for 18.5 and 22.5 percent, respectively, of apparent consumption; and by 1966 and 1967, reductions in imported steel had brought it back to 16 percent.[15] (See Table 47 below.)

2. A second important feature of Canada's steel industry in the postwar period has been the achievement of a relatively high ratio of capacity utilization by comparison with the steel industries in many other countries. Table 7 summarizes the performance for Canada, the ECSC countries, the United States, Japan, Great Britain, and the other EFTA countries. The figures for Canada emphasize that, except in recession years, the degree of capacity utilization has been relatively high compared to that of most of our international competitors. As the analysis in later chapters emphasizes,[16] the rise in worldwide excess steel capacity is a major factor in the current international steel-trade situation. It is important to remember that the Canadian industry, at least until very recently, did not live in this environment of excessive capacity. Here, the record in 1966 and 1967 changed, as the operating ratio

[15]However, recent years' import patterns, examined on a product-by-product basis, signal the beginnings of a new trend. Heretofore, Canadian steel imports reflected largely shortages in capacity or gaps in the Canadian steel-products structure; such imports were generally known as "deficit-covering" imports. By contrast, some of the imports appearing in recent years were directly in competition with available domestic production sources.
[16]See particularly pp. 54–5 below.

TABLE 7

RAW-STEEL-CAPACITY UTILIZATION, CANADA, ECSC, UNITED STATES, JAPAN, UNITED KINGDOM, AND OTHER EFTA COUNTRIES, 1955–66 (percentages)

	1955	1956	1957	1958	1959	1960	1961	1962	1963	1964	1965	1966
Canada	91.1	99.7	90.2	72.1	91.8	86.3	90.1	89.4	99.9	99.8	95.4	87.2
ECSC		96.1	93.9	85.9	89.6	95.5	91.7	87.5	83.3	90.0	84.2	78.4
United States	93.0	89.8	84.5	60.6	63.6	66.8	65.0	63.0	68.0	77.0	78.0	77.0
Japan	93.1	98.3	82.3	73.2	87.6	100.0	103.7	89.7	87.4	95.4	93.0	100.8
United Kingdom	98.2			83.6	85.0	94.1	83.2	74.0	78.0	87.5	87.0	78.8
Other EFTA countries	90.9			89.9		98.8	95.6	93.7	93.9	100.0	97.3	93.1
ECSC members:												
West Germany		97.8	95.2	83.7	89.4	96.5	90.7	85.6	79.5	91.2	80.9	
France		95.0	94.6	93.4	93.9	96.7	94.7	88.1	84.0	91.6	86.5	
Italy		92.6	91.5	80.1	84.3	94.3	93.0	91.4	92.5	83.7	84.6	
Netherlands		97.3	93.3	92.5	90.4	93.5	90.2	82.2	79.7	84.4	88.8	
Belgium		93.8	87.9	80.8	84.6	88.9	84.8	87.9	85.1	88.6	87.5	
Luxembourg		98.5	97.0	93.6	93.7	98.6	97.7	93.7	90.3	94.2	93.5	

Sources: Canada: Table 1.
ECSC and member countries: *Eisen und Stahl, Jahrbuch 1966*, pp. 10–11.
United States: American Iron and Steel Institute and U.S. Senate, *Steel Import Study*.
Japan: The Japan Iron and Steel Federation.
United Kingdom and other EFTA countries: Organisation for European Economic Co-operation and Organization for Economic Co-operation and Development.

of the industry fell to 87.2 percent in 1966 and to 82.1 percent in 1967.[17] General economic activity remained at high (though no longer sharply rising) levels, and steel consumption stabilized after several years of very rapid growth; under these circumstances the increased capacity of the Canadian steel industry could not be fully utilized. Combined with the continuation of price-competitive imports among a number of major product groups, this larger capacity has given rise to a new steel-market situation in Canada, more representative of the pressures that have been felt on a much greater scale in the U.S. steel market for a number of years. (The issues surrounding this new situation will be examined more fully in chapters 2 and 3.)

The U.S. steel industry's operating ratios have, in general, been the lowest for any of the countries covered in our comparisons. As the industry has not published official capacity figures since 1961, the data shown are based on private estimates made by the *Wall Street Journal* and are open to some doubts. In the ECSC, the operating ratio of steel fell below 90 percent in 1962 (the only previous lower rate of utilization was 90 percent in 1959) and has since then remained below 90 percent (except in 1964, when it was 90 percent exactly), falling to 78.4 percent in 1966. In contrast, the Japanese operating ratio has generally remained the highest of all of any of the large producing nations.

3. A third implication of the Canadian steel industry's rapid postwar progress arises in the financial performance of the industry. Generalizations and conclusions are a great deal more difficult in this sphere, but our analysis (see pages 50–52) indicates that by most of the accepted financial tests for which reasonably comparative data are available, the performance of the Canadian steel industry compares favourably with the performances of the industries of the large steel-producing nations.

4. Although volumes remain modest in relation to total Canadian steel output, exports of Canadian steel have been built up gradually in the postwar period. (For further details, see pages 87–88.)

D. CAPITAL-INVESTMENT TRENDS AND TECHNOLOGICAL PROGRESS

The rapid growth of the Canadian steel industry in the postwar period is reflected in its new investment-expenditure trends (Table 8). In the early postwar years, the industry's investments were relatively modest, averaging some $13 million annually during the years 1948 to 1950.[18] The surge since then can be illustrated by successive five-year averages. These were $48 million annually for the years 1951–55, $76 million annually from 1956 to 1960, and $129 million annually for the years 1961 to 1965. In 1966 new

[17]Both years are slightly affected by work stoppages at one of the companies.
[18]Separate figures for the primary iron and steel industry were first published in 1948.

TABLE 8

CANADIAN PRIMARY IRON AND STEEL INDUSTRY,
CAPITAL EXPENDITURES, 1948–67
(thousands of dollars)

	Construction	Machinery and equipment	Total
1948	7,282	12,011	19,293
1949	2,435	9,201	11,636
1950	1,704	5,225	6,929
1951	28,945	21,366	50,311
1952	20,520	52,394	72,914
1953	11,914	38,011	49,925
1954	6,239	27,300	33,539
1955	6,615	27,930	34,545
1956	7,613	54,083	61,696
1957	14,366	56,648	71,014
1958	15,420	40,433	55,853
1959	15,044	59,677	74,721
1960	23,789	90,975	114,764
1961	14,411	52,838	67,249
1962	20,898	91,979	112,877
1963	24,727	82,552	107,279
1964	36,600	169,468	206,068
1965	25,310	127,099	152,409
1966	35,100	175,460	210,560
1967[a]	21,480	94,517	115,997

Source: Department of Trade and Commerce, *Private and Public Investment in Canada*. For the years 1955–59, Standard Industrial Classification Code no. 325, *Primary Iron and Steel*, was used.
[a]Preliminary.

investment expenditures reached $211 million, and the preliminary total for 1967 declined to $116 million. Even after allowing for large increases in the prices of capital goods during the postwar period, a sharp acceleration in the rate of real capital investment emerges, particularly after 1950. These figures, incidentally, represent the expenditures of establishments classified only as iron and steel mills and exclude major investments made by the industry in iron ore mining and fabricating operations.

A more meaningful analysis of capital-investment trends is precluded by the lack of capital-stock statistics for the industry. DBS data on fixed-capital flows and on capital stocks for manufacturing industries from 1926 to 1960 group all the iron and steel products industries together,[19] and this classifica-

[19]See DBS, *Fixed Capital Flows and Stock, Manufacturing, Canada, 1926–1960*, cat. no. 13-523, Aug. 1966, and no. 13-522, *Methodology*, Feb. 1967.

tion is too broad to be of any appreciable value in obtaining an insight into capital-stock and capital-productivity trends of this industry.[20]

The degree to which the Canadian steel industry has adopted technological change and the speed with which the change was undertaken are criteria which can be examined in conjunction with the above capital-expenditure trends. Generally speaking, the growing scale of operations of the industry— ranging from increases in appropriately prepared raw materials to the enlargement of existing, and the provision of new, rolling mill facilities— allowed the industry to utilize the most modern techniques and equipment available, even though, in many spheres of the steel production process, the pace of technological advance was steady rather than spectacular. This description seems to fit progress in raw material preparation (ore beneficiation), blast furnace technology (larger blast furnaces, better prepared raw materials going into them, and expanded injection of fuels into the furnaces) and hot-rolling, cold-rolling, and finishing-mill operations, which have benefited significantly from the introduction of process computers and other instrumentation, wider and faster mills, and other quality-improving changes.[21]

In the relatively few instances of truly technological revolution, the Canadian record stands up well. The consensus among steel-industry experts is that the most significant single postwar technological change in the production processes for steel was the development of the basic oxygen furnace (BOF). The pre-World War II history of the research and invention processes is described in detail by Adams and Dirlam;[22] for present purposes it suffices to record that the Austrian firm VOEST (*Vereinigte Österreichische Eisen und Stahlwerke, A.G.*) successfully installed and began the first commercial oxygen process in the world in 1952. The Austrians referred to the technical process as the "L-D," which stands either for Linz-Dusenverfahren or for Linz-Donawitz, the location of the company's plant.[23] The first North American installation of the new process occurred in Canada at Dofasco's plant in 1954; later in the same year, an installation was made in the United States by one of the smaller companies—McLouth Steel in Detroit, Michigan.

[20]This is regrettable in the light of available information for the U.S. steel industry (see U.S. Senate, Committee on Finance, *Steel Import Study*, Washington, 1967, p. 175), indicating a doubling in the capital-output ratio of the U.S. steel industry during the postwar period, compared to a small decline for all manufacturing industries.
[21]Descriptions adopted from the *Steel Import Study*, pp. 168–70. See also, United Nations, Economic Commission for Europe, *Automation in the Iron and Steel Industry, 1965*.
[22]Walter Adams and Joel B. Dirlam, "Big Steel, Invention and Innovation," *Quarterly Journal of Economics*, LXXX, no. 2, May 1966, pp. 169–74.
[23]On this continent, it is variously known as the oxygen converter process, basic oxygen furnace process, BOP, or OSM. *Ibid.*, p. 174.

In Canada, the initial BOF capacity of Dofasco amounted to 350,000 tons in 1955, or 7.2 percent of total Canadian raw steel capacity in that year. Subsequent additions by Dofasco, and Algoma's heavy investment into the process, brought Canadian BOF capacity to 2.1 million tons in 1963 (26.0 percent of total capacity) and to more than 3.5 million tons in 1967 (30.5

TABLE 9

BOF STEEL PRODUCTION (OR CAPACITY), AS PERCENTAGE
OF TOTAL, SELECTED COUNTRIES, 1955–67

	Canada[a]	United States[b]	Japan[b]	ECSC[b]
1955	7.2	0.3[c]	4.3	
1956	6.7	0.4[c]	4.0	
1957	9.6	0.5[c]	3.6	
1958	12.0	1.5	6.8	1.1
1959	17.2	2.0	7.2	1.5
1960	21.8	3.4	11.9	2.2
1961	22.3	4.1	19.0	3.2
1962	23.7	5.6	30.6	4.8
1963	26.0	7.8	38.2	7.5
1964	28.4	12.2	44.2	12.6
1965	30.0	17.4	55.0	19.2
1966	31.5	25.3	62.6	23.4[a]
1967	30.5	32.7		

Sources: Canada: Table 1; United States: U.S. Senate, *Steel Import Study*, Table 92, p. 170, and *American Metal Market*, Jan. 26, 1968; Japan: Japan Iron and Steel Federation, *Statistical Yearbook for 1965*, pp. 28–9; ECSC: *Eisen und Stahl, Jahrbuch 1966*, p. 22.
[a]Capacity Jan. 1 each year.
[b]Production.
[c]Corrected.

percent of total capacity).[24] In international comparisons of steel efficiency, considerable significance has been attached to the degree of BOF capacity in relation to total raw steel capacity. Table 9 summarizes Canada's record, showing its early lead in the adaptation of the process—a lead which it has held over the ECSC and, until 1967, over the United States. The figures also illustrate the sharp rise of Japanese BOF capacity, with output produced by this process amounting to 62.6 percent of the total in 1966 (Table 9).

[24]For capacity details by company and in total, see Department of Energy, Mines and Resources, *Metallurgical Works in Canada, Primary Iron and Steel*, Operators List, part 1, Jan. 1967 (annual). Dofasco's entire raw steel production uses the BOF process and Algoma's ratio is 56 percent. Neither Stelco nor Dosco have BOF installations.

The extent to which the relatively slow adoption of the BOF process by the U.S. steel industry has affected its competitive position since the mid-1950s has been assessed as follows:

Other countries, particularly Japan, have a larger proportion of oxygen converters in relation to total steelmaking operations than does the United States. However, the vessels which were first installed in Europe and Japan constituted an expansion of the industry in those countries. Our expansion of basic steelmaking capacity took place in the early 1950s with larger open hearth furnaces and at that time the oxygen process had not been perfected to its present state. Consequently, the large open hearths which used oxygen were more productive than the oxygen converters of the early 1950s.[25]

The recent study for the Senate Finance Committee concluded on the basic significance of the BOF process as follows:

In recent years [1962–67] steel industry capital spending to a large degree has been directed toward the conversion process of hot metal to steel. Basic oxygen furnaces accounted for 25.3 percent of raw steel production in 1966, compared to 5.6 percent in 1962. . . . The rush in recent years to make steel by this method has been necessitated by the state of competition, both domestic and foreign. The basic oxygen process lowers the cost of production from $5 to $7 a ton and capital costs are approximately one-half that of the conventional open-hearth furnace; namely, $18 million versus $35 million. (Capital costs are also slightly lower than electric furnaces.)[26]

The second path-breaking technological change of our times in steelmaking is the continuous-casting process, which permits bypassing the ingot stage of the production process and going immediately from molten raw steel to semi-finished steel forms. With continuous casting, molten steel is cast directly into an open-end mold of the required cross-section, from which solidified steel is continuously withdrawn and cut to desired lengths. The product is a bloom, billet, or slab.

The development of continuous casting began after World War II and accelerated in the 1960s. The first continuous-casting unit in North America was installed in 1954 by Atlas Steels in Welland, Ontario. Table 10 lists the continuous-casting units installed since then or still under construction. By mid-1967 nine plants were reported to have continuous-casting equipment, with a combined annual capacity of 1.9 million tons, or 17 percent of total Canadian raw steel capacity.

One published estimate of the cost advantages obtainable from continuous

---

[25]William J. Hogan, S.J., "The Steel Import Problem: A Question of Quality and Price," *Thought*, XL, no. 159, Winter 1965, pp. 593–4.
[26]U.S. Senate, *Steel Import Study*, p. 169.

TABLE 10

STEEL CONTINUOUS CASTING IN CANADA AS OF APRIL, 1967

	Location	Starting date	Annual capacity[a]	Ladle capacity[a]	No. of molds	No. of strands	Type of mold	Type of steel cast	Capital cost ($ millions)
Algoma Steel	Sault Ste. Marie	1967	600,000 (2 machines)	110 110	4 2	4 2	curved curved	low alloy carbon	16
Atlas Steels (Rio Algom Mines Ltd.)	Welland Tracy, Que.	1954 1965	93,500 75,000 (nominal)	30.50 75	1 1	1 or 2 1 or 2	vertical curved	stainless, alloy stainless	— —
Dosco Steel Limited	Montreal	1965	150,000 (minimum)	38	1	4	compact, curved	carbon	2.2
Lake Ontario Steel	Whitby	1964	200,000	50	6	6	vertical[b]	carbon	—
Manitoba Rolling Mill (Dominion Bridge)	Selkirk	1966	160,000	—	2	4	compact, curved	carbon	—
Stelco	Edmonton	1962	110,000	20	1	2	vertical[b]	low alloy, carbon	1.2
Stelco	Hamilton	1966	350,000 (minimum)	90	1	6	compact, curved	carbon grades	9
Western Canada Steel	Vancouver	1963	100,000	30	1	3	vertical[b]	carbon	1
Burlington Steel	Hamilton	1967	—	—			low head	carbon	—
Newfoundland Steel	Octagon Pond	1966	60,000	28	2	2	straight	low alloy	—

Source: Department of Energy, Mines and Resources, *Primary Iron and Steel*, 1966.

[a] Net tons

[b] Bent before cutting.

casting puts the savings in operating costs at $4 per ton, resulting from a reduction in employment and other costs, a significant increase in yield, and a small offset from higher overhead costs.[27]

In the United States, continuous casting accounted for one percent of the steel processed in 1966 but may account for 25 percent by the mid-1970s.[28]

As can be seen from Table 10, three of the "Big Four" basic steel producers in Canada had installed continuous-casting facilities by 1967. A number of the smaller plants, including Atlas Steels, also adopted this process during the 1960s. In absolute terms, the rated capacity of Algoma's two machines that went into production in 1967 was largest, with 600,000 tons annually. Stelco was next, with an estimated 460,000 tons of capacity at Hamilton and Edmonton (where Premier Steel Mills was the second Canadian company to install the process in 1962). In 1965 Dosco brought in continuous-casting facilities at its Montreal works with a capacity of 150,000 tons.

Since continuous-casting techniques in their present stage of development are not suitable for rimming steels which are required for high surface quality in sheet production, the usefulness of the new process will not be the same for all producers. This is seen in the differences in the rates of adoption of Algoma, Atlas, Dosco, and Lake Ontario Steel, compared to Stelco and Dofasco. (The latter has no continuous-casting facilities.)

E. EMPLOYMENT, WAGES, AND TRENDS IN LABOUR PRODUCTIVITY

Total employment in the primary iron and steel industry has risen from approximately 30,000 persons in the early postwar years to 35,000 at the end of the 1950s and nearly 46,000 in 1966. Production and other hourly rated workers typically account for more than 80 percent of total employment in the industry. The standard work week for hourly rated wage earners declined from 44 hours at the end of World War II to 40 hours in the early 1950s. Since that time there have been cyclical fluctuations around the 40-hour-week base, with actual averages falling below 40 hours in recession years and typically ranging between 40 and 41 hours per week at other times. In 1965 and 1966, average weekly hours of hourly rated employees in iron and steel mills (SIC 291) were 40.8 and 40.3, respectively.

Average hourly earnings of production workers in the primary iron and steel industry in Canada have risen from 83 cents per hour in 1946 to an estimated $3.11 per hour in 1967. Annual figures for the period 1951 to

[27]U.S. Senate, *Steel Import Study*, p. 135. Estimates prepared by L. F. Rothschild & Company in 1965 with specific reference to the Republic Steel Corporation.
[28]*Ibid.*, p. 170.

TABLE 11

PRIMARY IRON AND STEEL INDUSTRY,
AVERAGE HOURLY EARNINGS, CANADA
AND UNITED STATES 1951–67

	Canada[a] ($ Canadian)	United States[b] ($ U.S.)
1951	1.43	1.89
1952	1.60	1.99
1953	1.70	2.16
1954	1.71	2.20
1955	1.81	2.37
1956	1.97	2.52
1957	2.15	2.68
1958	2.25	2.88
1959	2.36	3.06
1960	2.44	3.04
1961	2.54	3.16
1962	2.60	3.25
1963	2.67	3.31
1964	2.71	3.36
1965	2.83	3.42
1966	2.94	3.53
1967	3.11	3.57

Sources: U.S. Bureau of Labor Statistics,
Monthly Labor Review. DBS, *Man-Hours
and Hourly Earnings*, cat. nos. 72-003,
72-202, 72-204.
[a]Primary iron and steel.
[b]Blast furnace and basic steel products.

1967 are shown in Table 11. The definition of average hourly earnings is as follows:

1. The gross wages of hourly rated employees, before deductions for taxes and unemployment insurance.
2. Payments for overtime work, incentive or productive and cost-of-living bonuses paid at regular intervals, and amounts credited to wage earners on leave without pay.
3. Excluded are infrequent bonuses, employers' contributions to welfare funds such as workmen's compensation, unemployment insurance, and pension and medical plans.[29]

Data expressing the hourly costs for the entire wage package, including fringe benefits, are not published in Canada, and this precludes a complete view of trends in total wage costs. Judging from data available for the U.S. steel industry, total employment costs have risen significantly faster than

[29]DBS, *Review of Man-Hours and Hourly Earnings*, cat. no. 72-202, explanatory notes.

hourly earnings as more extensive fringe benefits have become an increasingly important goal of organized labour in the postwar period. The U.S. data show an increase in average hourly earnings from $1.28 in 1946 to $3.53 in 1966, an increase of $2.25, or 176 percent. By comparison, total employment costs per hour, reported by the American Iron and Steel Institute, rose from $1.40 to $4.63 in the same interval,[30] or by $3.23 per hour, or 231 percent. The hourly value of fringe benefits thus amounted to $0.12 in 1946, compared to $1.10 in 1966.

Returning to the average hourly earnings data, the ratio of steel wages in Canada to those in the United States increased from 65 percent in 1946 to 87 percent in 1967, ignoring changes in the official exchange rate. At the time of the 1966 Canadian contract settlements, it was reported that the wage of a steel worker in Ontario (who currently has a margin of approximately 3.5 percent above the Canadian average) would come close to the U.S. average under existing contract provisions. This comparison, of course, ignores exchange rate and purchasing power differences and implies approximately identical packages of non-wage benefits.

The data on labour productivity[31] trends in the Canadian steel industry (Table 12), based on estimates of labour input and two alternative measurements of output,[32] show that output per man-hour has been rising at an annual rate of close to 6 percent since 1949.[33] Data calculated in the Bank of Nova Scotia study for the period 1938–49 show that, in spite of the surge in output in this period, output per man-hour rose only nominally in that interval.[34]

As a base for long-term trend calculations in steel productivity, 1949 has the drawback of having been a relatively static year (with production unchanged at 3.2 million tons of raw steel and an operating ratio of 89.8 percent) for the Canadian industry. However, the choice of another early postwar base would not materially affect the results; and in addition, the

[30]The American Iron and Steel Institute data on "pay for hours worked" show small variations from the Bureau of Labor Statistics data on hourly earnings. The Institute's measurements of "total employment costs per hour" are compared here with BLS hourly-earnings series.
[31]The DBS reports it has a detailed study under way on productivity in the steel industry. See DBS, *Productivity Trends in Industry*, Report no. 1, 1966, foreword.
[32]Ingots and castings in net tons, and the index of industrial production for primary iron and steel mills.
[33]The calculations shown update the statistics developed by the late Dr. Lucy Morgan in the Bank of Nova Scotia's study, *The Canadian Primary Iron and Steel Industry*, for the (Gordon) Royal Commission on Canada's Economic Prospects, Oct. 1956, Table 18, p. 76.
[34]From an average of 94.7 in the years 1938–40 to 100 in 1949 (1949 = 100), *ibid.*, p. 76.

TABLE 12

CANADIAN PRIMARY IRON AND STEEL INDUSTRY, GENERAL MEASURES OF PRODUCTIVITY, 1953–66

(all indexes on basis of 1949 = 100)

	(1) Production of ingots and castings (000 net tons)	(2) Total man-hours paid for (000)	(3) Index of total man-hours paid for	(4) Production of ingots and castings per man-hour (net tons) (1 ÷ 2)	(5) Index of production of ingots and castings per man-hour	(6) Index of industrial production, primary iron and steel	(7) Index of net value added per man-hour (6 ÷ 3)
1953	4,116	64,359	106.0	.0640	122.1	127.0	119.8
1954	3,195	51,080	84.1	.0625	119.3	109.2	129.8
1955	4,535	62,787	103.4	.0722	137.8	155.8	150.7
1956	5,302	69,056	113.7	.0768	146.6	190.3	167.4
1957	5,038	65,600	108.0	.0768	146.6	166.6	154.3
1958	4,345	52,257	86.1	.0831	158.6	138.7	161.1
1959	5,900	63,569	104.7	.0928	177.1	189.4	180.9
1960	5,809	61,342	101.0	.0947	180.7	185.1	183.3
1961	6,467	59,336	97.7	.1090	208.0	200.8	205.5
1962	7,174	63,319	104.3	.1133	216.2	224.8	215.5
1963	8,190	66,924	110.2	.1224	233.6	255.4	231.8
1964	9,131	73,408	120.9	.1244	237.4	291.2	240.9
1965	10,029	77,202	127.2	.1299	247.9	320.0	251.6
1966	10,003	80,205	132.1	.1247	238.0	324.8	245.9

Sources: Ingot and castings production: DBS, *Primary Iron and Steel*, cat. no. 41-001.
Total man-hours paid: up to 1960, computed from DBS, *Review of Man-Hours and Hourly Earnings 1945–64*, cat. no. 72-202, and *Iron and Steel Mills*, cat. no. 41-203; after 1961, *Iron and Steel Mills* (annual), figure on hours paid for as published. Index of industrial production, primary iron and steel: DBS, *Index of Industrial Production*, cat. no. 61-005.

1949 base permits comparisons (shown in Table 13) with selected aggregate productivity indexes.

Although international comparisons of trends in output per man-hour move us to an area of greater conceptual and statistical problems, it is significant that the Canadian estimates compare favourably with most of the countries for which output-per-man-hour data are available. Table 14 shows output-per-man-hour data for the United States, the individual ECSC countries, Japan, and the United Kingdom for the years 1955, 1960, and

TABLE 13

1966 INDEXES OF OUTPUT PER MAN-HOUR, CANADA
(1949 = 100)

Primary iron and steel	245.9
Non-agricultural goods-producing industries	202.2
Manufacturing	191.5

Sources: Table 12 (for steel) and DBS, *Aggregate Productivity Trends, 1946-66*, cat. no. 14-201.

1965. For comparative purposes the Canadian estimates (developed in Table 12) have been added, showing that in the decade 1955–65 the output-per-man-hour gain of 67 percent exceeded that of the United States (25 percent) and of the United Kingdom (39 percent), was a shade below that of the ECSC group (71 percent), and much smaller than the Japanese gain (149 percent).[35] Compared to individual ECSC countries, the Canadian increase was about the same as that of France, the Netherlands, and Belgium, exceeded Luxembourg and West Germany, but did not match the sharp gains of Italy. The period from 1960 to 1965 turns the Canadian-ECSC comparison in favour of Canada (37 percent, compared to 24 percent). This is understandable in the light of some of the problems that the industries within the ECSC began to encounter in the 1960s, compared to the prosperity and sharp expansion of the Canadian industry between 1961 and 1965.

A second, somewhat longer view of the trends in output per man-hour in the steel industries of Canada, the United States, and the United Kingdom appears in Figure 3. The annual rate of gain for the Canadian industry is 5.5 percent for the years 1947–66,[36] and it clearly exceeds the U.S. gain,

[35]These results appear more meaningful than the 1960–65 comparisons, which have an unsuitable starting point for the United States and Canada because of the recessions in general business activity.
[36]The U.S. calculations of a 1.7 percent trend rate are based on 1947–66. We have used the same starting point for Canada, though the output-per-man-hour index for 1947 (106.0) is irregularly high by comparison to adjacent years (1946 = 83.7 and 1948 = 96.7).

TABLE 14

COMPARISON OF FINISHED-STEEL OUTPUT PER MAN-HOUR,
SELECTED COUNTRIES

Country	Year	Output per man-hour (1955 = 100)	Output per man-hour (1960 = 100)
United Kingdom	1955	100	85
	1960	118	100
	1965	139	118
West Germany	1955	100	73
	1960	137	100
	1965	158	115
France	1955	100	74
	1960	134	100
	1965	169	126
Italy	1955	100	54
	1960	187	100
	1965	255	137
Netherlands	1955	100	73
	1960	136	100
	1965	168	124
Belgium	1955	100	81
	1960	123	100
	1965	166	135
Luxembourg	1955	100	79
	1960	126	100
	1965	147	117
ECSC	1955	100	72
	1960	139	100
	1965	171	124
United States	1955	100	96
	1960	104	100
	1965	125	120
Japan	1955	100	65
	1960	154	100
	1965	249	162
Canada	1955	100	82
	1960	122	100
	1965	167	137

Sources: Canada: Table 12. Other countries: U.S. Senate, *Steel Import Study*, Table 103, p. 183. From 1955–65 the output per man-hour for the United States, as prepared by BLS, increased about 15 percent for all employees and 20 percent for production workers only, instead of the 25 percent shown here. This table, except for the Canadian data (added by the author), was prepared by the British Iron and Steel Board (BISB) but has not been published. It is believed that the data used by the BISB are internally consistent, but they are obviously calculated by a different method.

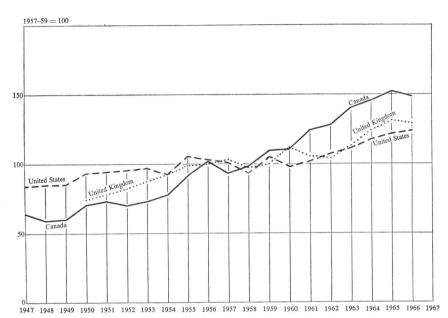

Figure 3   Indexes of Output per Man-hour, Steel Industries of Canada, the United States, and the United Kingdom, 1947–66 (1957–59 = 100).

Sources: for U.K.: *Steel Import Study*, p. 211; for U.S.: *ibid.*, p. 166; for Canada: Table 12, col. 7.

calculated at 1.7 percent.[37] The British industry's figures cover the years 1950 to 1966 and show an annual gain of 3.5 percent.

Another comparison of labour productivity can be made with the help of the American Iron and Steel Institute (AISI) data supplied for the Senate Finance Committee study. The comparisons relate to output of finished steel (in tons) produced per 1,000 man-hours in 1957 and 1966. Index numbers are shown in Table 15, since absolute output levels are not comparable among various countries because of differences in the product-mix of the steel industries. We have added the Canadian data (using total shipments of rolling mill products as shown in Table 3) for comparison; and on this basis the annual rate of gain for the Canadian industry in the period 1957–66 amounted to 4.8 percent, compared to 2.0 percent for the United States, 11.7 percent for Japan, and 4.6 percent for the ECSC group.

F. PRICE TRENDS

A study seeking to explain the structure and shifts in the international trade of particular products has to choose among a number of basic explanatory

[37]Both based on least-squares trend of logarithms of the index numbers, 1947 to 1966. See U.S. Senate, *Steel Import Study*, Table 89, p. 166.

TABLE 15
1966 INDEXES OF OUTPUT OF FINISHED-STEEL PRODUCTS
PER 1,000 MAN-HOURS, SELECTED COUNTRIES
(1957 = 100)

	Canada	United States	Japan	ECSC
1957	100	100	100	100
1966	152	120	270	150
Annual rate of gain (percent)	4.8	2.0	11.7	4.6

Sources: Canada: Tables 3 and 12. Other countries: U.S. Senate, *Steel Import Study*, p. 182.

factors. The "real side" of the equation is levels and changes in total productivity and costs, which, if fully documented, should give an insight into absolute and comparative advantage in international trade of a particular product. In the absence of reliable cost information for the Canadian and other steel industries, and with a meagre amount of productivity statistics, our analysis of the competitive position of the Canadian steel industry falls back on the next best proxy indicator—a comparison of steel-price trends.

Recent literature on the subject of international competition has suggested that actual prices rather than costs may be more relevant to an explanation of shifts in trade patterns, particularly for manufactured products, where substitutability is less than perfect and identical price changes are not as likely as in the case of trade in standard raw materials.[38] In addition, other practical advantages pertain to the use of price rather than cost data:
1. The concept of price, although not without difficulties, is generally more objective and less likely to vary from one source to another.[39]
2. It is easier to obtain information about prices than about costs, not only because many sellers are more willing to provide price than cost information, but also because price information can be supplied by buyers. Moreover, cost data can be built up only for whole plants, companies, or groups of commodities, rather than for precisely specified individual commodities. International cost comparisons for individual products would be distorted by the diversity in methods of allocating costs in different firms and countries.[40]

In our case, the argument for a price analysis is even more emphatic, since the usual gap in cost data is more pronounced for the steel industry than

[38]Irving Kravis and others, "Measuring International Price Competitiveness: A Preliminary Report," National Bureau of Economic Research, *Occasional Paper 94*, 1965, p. 20.
[39]*Ibid.*, p. 21.
[40]*Ibid.*

in many other instances. The analysis presented below begins with an assessment of the competitiveness of the Canadian steel industry in the North American market by means of a detailed comparison of Canadian and U.S. steel prices in the postwar period. In chapter 3, the price data available from offshore steel producers are added for comparison.

North American steel prices. The elements that make up the price of steel to a consumer at a given location in the North American market include:

1. A base-price quotation, which is the price at which the producer is willing to sell f.o.b. mill at his production point. There are quotations for broad categories of products such as bars, sheet, plate, and all structurals. "This system of base prices is almost universally followed, and since the categories covered by the base prices are usually of uniform coverage, it is possible to compare base prices at various mills, both in Canada and abroad, on a reasonably comparable basis."[41] Next there are charges for extras, including size and quality specifications, which, combined with the base price, give a "net" price. For example, the base price of a merchant carbon steel bar at Sault Ste. Marie, Ontario, in June, 1967, was $5.65 per hundred pounds, or $113 per net ton. Specified as 2 × 2 × ¼" angles of mild steel, the net price becomes $132 per ton. Although subsequent comparisons in this study generally use quotations for basic products without extras, it should be remembered that actual transaction prices will vary according to the extras that are usually included in a particular transaction. The following presentation documents the trends in North American steel prices by means of the base-price quotations, updating the compilations by the Bank of Nova Scotia study up to the mid-1950s for the last twelve years.

Since our price comparisons are international, the exchange rate for the Canadian dollar is taken into account. All price quotations are thus converted into Canadian dollars, and the comparisons illustrate the extent to which changes in the exchange rate have affected the competitive position of foreign steel in Canadian markets and vice-versa.

2. The base-price quotations are f.o.b. mill, to which the buyer has to add the cost of transportation to his location in order to arrive at the delivered price of steel. Unless a steel consumer is close to a mill, the freight costs can be a significant component in the delivered price of steel.[42] As we are dealing with a homogeneous product, a given user will look to the steel plant nearest to him as a source of supply, in order to minimize his total delivered costs; any mill wishing to compete outside the territory in which it has a "natural"

---

[41]Tariff Board, *Report . . . Respecting Basic Iron and Steel Products, Reference No. 118*, Ottawa, Feb. 1957, p. 44.
[42]This is true particularly in Canada, where there are only a few steel-production points and many spread-out consumption points.

freight advantage would have to absorb freight costs in order to compete at destinations outside this territory.

In terms of Canadian and U.S. prices only, the delivered price for a given customer is made up of the base price (plus extras) and the cost of the most economical method of transportation from the nearest production mill to the consumer. Historically, this has meant the computation of rail freight rates from the base point to the delivery point.[43] From a practical standpoint of current Canadian computations, one must also take into account "agreed charges" among steel mills and the railways, and truck rates, as the latter form of transportation has become highly competitive over shorter hauls.

In addition, with the rising penetration of North American (particularly U.S.) steel markets by offshore suppliers, competitive assessments must also take into account ocean shipping rates (see page 100 below), which become a major element in determining the competitiveness of offshore steel.
3. The next variable in an international comparison of prices is customs tariff rates. The tariff is an important consideration in our commercial policy analysis in chapter 3. In the international price comparisons in this chapter, the rates of the Canadian customs tariff are incorporated into foreign steel quotations (along with freight costs), in order to arrive at full delivered prices of steel in the Canadian market.

Our analysis of the price competitiveness of Canadian steel takes all the above factors into account. The data available permit a detailed evaluation of comparative Canadian-U.S. price trends, as all the dimensions entering final price determination are unambiguous and readily ascertainable. By comparison, the analysis relating to prices of offshore producers is blurred by uncertainty as to both quotations and ocean-transport freight costs.

Long-term price trends. The Tariff Board report includes historical material on Canadian steel prices for the period 1937 to 1956, showing that Canadian base prices were substantially higher than corresponding U.S. base prices in the prewar period.[44] For example, in 1937 the Canadian base price for hot-rolled bars was more than 8 percent above the U.S. price; similarly, the differentials for hot-rolled plate and hot-rolled sheet amounted to almost 21 percent in each case.[45] By the mid-1950s, Canadian base prices were still higher than those in the United States, in a range from 4 percent for hot-rolled sheets to 11 percent for plate.

A more detailed view of recent trends in Canadian and U.S. steel base

[43]When the single-basing-point system ("Pittsburgh Plus") was in use in the United States, all freight computations were based on Pittsburgh, leading either to "phantom" freight or freight absorption as far as mills not located at Pittsburgh were concerned.
[44]Tariff Board, *Report Respecting Basic Iron and Steel Products,* p. 44.
[45]*Ibid.*

prices is obtained in Table 16; we have selected products for comparison which are representative of broad categories of rolling mill products and enter international steel trade in large volumes.

As an example of changes in relative Canadian-U.S. base prices, the following discussion uses hot-rolled carbon merchant bars, for which the prewar (1937) difference in Canadian-U.S. base prices amounted to more than 8 percent, the Canadian base price being the higher. By 1947 this differential had declined to 4 percent;[46] neither of these comparisons is materially altered by an adjustment for the exchange rate, as the U.S. and the Canadian dollars exchanged at par in both years.

Annual data for the years 1954 to 1968 are shown in Table 16; the quotations are base prices stated in Canadian dollars as of the beginning of every year. To emphasize the influence of exchange rate changes, the U.S. base prices in U.S. dollars are also shown. At the beginning of 1955 the Canadian base price was still 7 percent higher, but steel-price increases during the years 1955 to 1957 were smaller in Canada than in the United States and during 1958 were confined solely to the United States. As a result, the historical differential between Canadian and U.S. base prices was eliminated.

U.S. base prices increased by $7.00 per ton in 1955, $8.50 per ton in 1956, $7.00 per ton in 1957, and $5.00 per ton in 1958, for a total increase of $27.50 per ton. By comparison, the Hamilton, Ontario, base price for carbon merchant bars, which had started in 1955 at $92.00 per ton, $6.00 per ton above the corresponding Pittsburgh price ($7.20 after adjustment for exchange rate differences), increased by $7.00 per ton in 1955, $4.00 per ton in 1956, $5.00 per ton in 1957, and did not change at all in 1958, thus bringing the 1955 to 1958 total increase to $16 per ton. As a result, base prices in respective currencies were virtually identical at the beginning of 1958, and only the premium on the Canadian dollar resulted in a comparatively lower U.S. base price. A year later the further rise in U.S. base prices resulted in virtually identical prices after exchange rate adjustments.

From 1959 to 1963 the comparisons afford the luxury of observing the impact of, first, the reduced premium on the Canadian dollar and, later on, devaluation. At the beginning of 1959, the price spread in favour of the Canadian base amounted to $1.00 per ton (mainly as the result of the $5.00-per-ton increase in the U.S. price during 1958); by January, 1963, this had increased to $14.60 per ton as the result of devaluation. Price changes in recent years in both countries have been relatively small; in Canada there was a $5.00-per-ton increase in early 1966, while U.S. base prices went up by $5.00 per ton in October, 1963; down by $1.00 per ton in May, 1966; and up again by $3.00 per ton in September, 1967. At the end of 1967, the

46*Ibid.*

TABLE 16

COMPARISON OF BASE PRICES OF SELECTED STEEL PRODUCTS, CANADA AND UNITED STATES,[a] AS AT JANUARY, 1954–68
(dollars per hundred pounds)

	1954	1955	1956	1957	1958	1959	1960	1961	1962	1963	1964	1965	1966	1967	1968
Structural steel shapes, carbon															
U.S. (U.S. $)	4.10	4.25	4.60	5.00	5.28	5.50	5.50	5.50	5.50	5.50	5.70	5.70	5.70	5.85	5.85
U.S. (Can. $)	3.99	4.19	4.53	4.79	5.12	5.27	5.33	5.57	5.88	5.93	6.15	6.14	6.14	6.31	6.32
Canada-Sault Ste. Marie[b]	4.60	4.60	4.80	5.05	5.30	5.50	5.50	5.50	5.50	5.50	5.50	5.50	5.75	5.95	5.95
Steel plate, carbon															
U.S. (U.S. $)	4.10	4.23	4.50	4.85	5.12	5.30	5.30	5.30	5.30	5.30	5.55	5.55	5.55	5.55	5.75
U.S. (Can. $)	3.99	4.17	4.43	4.65	4.97	5.08	5.14	5.37	5.67	5.72	5.99	5.98	5.98	5.98	6.21
Hamilton[c]	4.60	4.95	4.95	5.25	5.45	5.45	5.45	5.45	5.45	5.45	5.45	5.45	5.45	5.45	5.45
Hot-rolled sheet, carbon															
U.S. (18-gauge and over) (U.S. $)	3.93	4.15	4.33	4.68	4.93	5.10	5.10	5.10	5.10	5.10	5.30	5.30	5.30	5.45	5.4
U.S. (Can. $)	3.82	4.09	4.26	4.49	4.79	4.89	4.95	5.17	5.45	5.50	5.72	5.71	5.71	5.88	5.89
Hamilton (over .080)	4.25	4.25	4.30	4.60	5.00	5.00	5.00	4.95	4.95	4.95	4.95	5.15	5.15	5.35	5.35
Cold-rolled sheet															
U.S. (U.S. $)	4.78	4.95	5.33	5.75	6.05	6.28	6.28	6.28	6.28	6.28	6.53	6.53	6.68	6.68	6.93
U.S. (Can. $)	4.65	4.88	5.25	5.51	5.87	6.02	6.09	6.36	6.71	6.77	7.04	7.04	7.04	7.20	7.48
Hamilton	5.10	5.10	5.25	6.05	6.35	6.35	6.35	6.35	6.35	6.35	6.35	6.35	6.60	6.80	6.80
Merchant bars, carbon															
U.S. (U.S. $)	4.15	4.30	4.65	5.08	5.43	5.68	5.68	5.68	5.68	5.68	5.93	5.93	5.93	5.88	6.03
U.S. (Can. $)	4.04	4.24	4.58	4.87	5.27	5.45	5.51	5.75	6.07	6.13	6.40	6.39	6.39	6.34	6.51
Canada-Hamilton	4.60	4.60	4.95	5.15	5.40	5.40	5.40	5.40	5.40	5.40	5.40	5.40	5.65	5.65	5.65

Sources: *Iron Age* and the Algoma Steel Corporation, Limited.

Note: U.S. prices have been converted to Canadian funds at the closing spot rates of the previous year.

[a]U.S. prices are Pittsburgh base prices.

[b]The Hamilton base price has been slightly lower since 1958. In Jan. 1968 it was $5.65 per hundred pounds.

[c]Up to 1959 Hamilton only; from 1959 on, Sault Ste. Marie supplied sheared mill steel plate a' identical mill base price as Hamilton.

Canadian-U.S. base-price differential thus amounted to $17.20 per net ton. The divergence in price trends in the period 1955 to 1967 has thus had a drastic impact upon the relative prices in this example. In terms of the over-all competitive implications, the "swing" amounted to more than 20 percent, with the ratio of the Canadian base relative to the U.S. price falling from 108.5 to 86.8. The contributions of actual price changes and exchange rate movements are shown in Table 17.

TABLE 17

BASE-PRICE CHANGES, CARBON MERCHANT BARS, CANADA AND
UNITED STATES, JANUARY, 1955, TO JANUARY, 1968

Base-price changes, January, 1955, to January, 1968:	
U.S. price change in U.S. dollars per ton—$34.60	
U.S. price change in Canadian dollars per ton	$45.40
Canadian price change in Canadian dollars per ton	21.00
Change in Canada's favour	$24.40
Canadian-U.S. base-price differentials (in Canadian dollars):	
January, 1955. Differential in U.S.'s favour	$ 7.20
January, 1968. Differential in Canada's favour	17.20
Change in Canada's favour	$24.40

The comparative price trends in base prices of other important categories of rolling mill products—structurals, plate, hot- and cold-rolled sheets—can be seen in Table 16. The resulting relative price movements between Canadian and U.S. base prices are summarized in Table 18, which divides the impact of differences in actual price changes and exchange rate movements. For the five product groups included, Canadian base prices were between 4 and 19 percent above the U.S. base prices in January, 1955; by comparison, they were in a range between 6 and 13 percent lower in January, 1968.

The inclusion of extras in both Canadian and U.S. base prices, as shown in Table 19, moderately reduces the Canadian advantage. For example, in the case of hot-rolled sheets, the Canadian-U.S. differential of 9.2 percent in terms of base prices adjusted for the exchange rate appears as 8.4 percent once the hot-rolled sheets are specified as commercial-quality sheets 60 × 0.1345 × 240″. Similarly, base-price differences for hot-rolled carbon bars, which show Canadian prices 13.2 percent below corresponding U.S. prices, reduce to 10.1 percent once the hot-rolled carbon bars are specified as 2 × 2 × ¼″ angles, mild steel.[47]

[47]The absolute charge for the "extra" involved is $19 per ton in respective Canadian and U.S. dollars.

TABLE 18

CANADIAN-U.S. BASE-PRICE DIFFERENTIALS AND CHANGES, SELECTED STEEL PRODUCTS,
JANUARY, 1955, TO JANUARY, 1968
(dollars per net ton)

	Structurals	Plate	Hot-rolled sheets	Cold-rolled sheets	Carbon bars
Canadian-U.S. base-price differentials (Can. $):					
January, 1955	+8.20	+15.60	+ 3.20	+ 4.40	+ 7.20
January, 1968	−7.40	−15.20	−10.80	−13.60	−17.20
Decline in Canadian price relative to U.S.	15.60	30.80	14.00	18.00	24.40
Ratio of Canadian base price to U.S. base price (Can. $):					
January, 1955	109.8	118.7	103.9	104.5	108.5
January, 1968	94.1	87.8	90.8	90.9	86.8
Source of decline in Canadian base prices relative to U.S. prices (Can. $):					
Price changes	5.00	20.40	4.00	5.60	13.60
Exchange rate movements	10.60	10.40	10.00	12.40	10.80
	15.60	30.80	14.00	18.00	24.40

Source: Computed from Table 16.

The Canadian tariff on steel rolling mill products acts as a further factor in magnifying the comparative price advantage for Canadian vis-à-vis U.S. steel in the Canadian market. For four of the five product groups discussed above—hot-rolled bars, structural shapes, hot-rolled plates, and hot-rolled sheets and strip—the MFN rate is 10 percent and will not be affected by the Kennedy round agreement. The tariff rate for cold-rolled sheets and strip is at present 15 percent and will be reduced to 12½ percent following implementation of the Kennedy round agreement. The Canadian and other large producing nations' steel tariffs are discussed below on pages 108–18.

The final element to be taken into account in this comparative price analysis is freight costs. Because of the relatively low value and high weight of steel and the fewness of production points relative to consumption points, the inclusion of transportation costs in the pricing system of the industry has historically been a major factor in the price policy of the industry. For present purposes we intend to determine to what extent freight costs affect the competitive position of Canadian steel in the domestic market. As examples, we are using freight-cost data for Toronto and Montreal in the east and Vancouver in western Canada.

The major determining factor of freight cost in the Toronto steel market (as of the summer of 1967) was a truck rate of 11 cents per hundred pounds applicable to all rolling mill products shipped from Hamilton. By comparison, the rail rate (with a 70,000-pound minimum) applicable to all rolling mill products shipped from Buffalo (where the Lackawanna division of Bethlehem Steel Corporation is the nearest U.S. plant that could serve the Toronto area market) is 44 cents per hundred pounds. From Pittsburgh, Pennsylvania, the rate rises sharply to 80 cents per hundred pounds. Thus, in the Toronto market, the nearest U.S. plant faces a freight disadvantage of $6.60 per ton of rolling mill product, compared to the Hamilton, Ontario, steel mills. This is about 5 percent of the Canadian base price for all the products shown on Table 19, with the exception of cold-rolled sheets (where the disadvantage is approximately 4½ percent). These figures illustrate the extent to which the nearest competing mill in the United States would have to absorb freight in delivering rolling mill products to Toronto destinations. A similar locational disadvantage applies to the Algoma Steel Corporation mill at Sault Ste. Marie, which, as the data show, faces a freight-cost disadvantage of either $7.80 per ton based on truck rates or $5.20 per ton based on a rail rate with a minimum of 140,000 pounds.

In the Montreal market, Dosco's plant provides free delivery to local users of hot-rolled bars and hot- and cold-rolled sheets.[48] For the latter two products, Dosco's base price is higher than that of the competing mills at Hamilton and Sault Ste. Marie, and this partly eliminates the freight-cost disadvantage of the other domestic mills.[49] For the eastern Canadian producers the current rail rates with a 120,000-pound minimum are $8.40 per ton from Hamilton and $11.10 per ton from Sault Ste. Marie; by comparison, the nearest U.S. eastern producer in Buffalo faces a $17.20-per-ton rail charge, which rises sharply for delivery from Pittsburgh to $25.60 per ton.

These figures illustrate the degree to which differences in overland transportation costs tend to add to the advantages that lower base prices and the tariff already give domestic mills in Canada's major eastern market locations. The present study does not attempt to produce a more detailed model showing freight-cost differentials at other locations, but a similar advantage exists throughout the Atlantic provinces (which are small consumers), the rest of Quebec, and large portions of the Ontario market. Southwestern Ontario, particularly Windsor, is an exception, as steel mills in the Detroit area would face a freight-cost advantage relative to Hamilton or Sault Ste. Marie.

Although the large western U.S. plants at Fontana, California, and Geneva,

[48]Among the products in our examples, Dosco does not produce heavy structurals or plate.
[49]Thus Hamilton and Sault Ste. Marie have to absorb less than the entire freight costs that they incur in selling into Montreal by reason of the relatively higher Dosco base price at destination.

TABLE 19

COMPARISON OF CANADIAN AND U.S. LAID-DOWN PRICES OF SELECTED STEEL PRODUCTS AT TORONTO AS OF AUGUST, 1967
(dollars per hundred pounds)

	Price		Duty	Freight to Toronto	Laid-down price	Canadian-U.S. laid-down price differential (amount by which Canadian laid-down price is lower)
	U.S. funds	Canadian funds				
Bars, carbon, hot-rolled						
2 × 2 × 1/4″ angles—mild steel:						
U.S., ex Buffalo	6.83	7.34	.73	.44[a]	8.51	
Canadian, ex Hamilton		6.60		.11[b]	6.71	1.80
Canadian, ex Sault Ste. Marie		6.60		.50[b]	7.10	1.41
Canadian, ex Sault Ste. Marie		6.60		.37[c]	6.97	1.54
Light structurals						
4 × 4 × 5/16″ angles—mild steel:						
U.S., ex Buffalo	6.55	7.04	.70	.44[a]	8.18	
U.S., ex Pittsburgh	6.55	7.04	.70	.80[a]	8.54	
Canadian, ex Hamilton		6.25		.11[b]	6.36	1.82* 2.18†
Canadian, ex Sault Ste. Marie		6.55		.50[b]	7.05	1.13* 1.49†
Canadian, ex Sault Ste. Marie		6.55		.37[c]	6.92	1.26* 1.62†
Heavy structurals						
12″ × 27# WF-ASTM A-7:						
U.S., ex Buffalo	6.45	6.93	.69	.44[a]	8.06	
U.S., ex Pittsburgh	6.45	6.93	.69	.80[a]	8.42	
Canadian, ex Sault Ste. Marie	6.45	6.45		.50[b]	6.95	1.11* 1.47†
Plate, carbon						
72 × 3/8 × 240″—mild steel:						
U.S., ex Pittsburgh	6.10	6.56	.66	.80[a]	8.02	
Canadian, ex Hamilton		5.90		.11[b]	6.01	2.01
Canadian, ex Sault Ste. Marie		5.90		.50[b]	6.40	1.62
Canadian, ex Sault Ste. Marie		5.90		.37[c]	6.27	1.75

TABLE 19 (continued)

| | Price | | | | | Canadian–U.S. laid-down price differential |
	U.S. funds	Canadian funds	Duty	Freight to Toronto	Laid-down price	(amount by which Canadian laid-down price is lower)
Plate for agricultural implements						
14 × 5/16 × 120″ U.M. Plate SAE 1025:						
U.S., ex Pittsburgh	7.05	7.58	free	.80[a]	8.38	
Canadian, ex Hamilton		6.95		.11[b]	7.06	1.32
Canadian, ex Sault Ste. Marie		6.95		.50[b]	7.45	.93
Canadian, ex Sault Ste. Marie		6.95		.37[c]	7.32	1.06
Sheet, hot-rolled						
60 × .1345 × 240″—comm. qual.:						
U.S., ex Buffalo	6.45	6.93	.69	.44[a]	8.06	
Canadian, ex Hamilton		6.35		.11[b]	6.46	1.60
Canadian, ex Sault Ste. Marie		6.20		.50[b]	6.70	1.36
Canadian, ex Sault Ste. Marie		6.20		.37[c]	6.57	1.49
Sheet, cold-rolled						
48 × .0299 × 120″—comm. qual.:						
U.S., ex Buffalo	7.78	8.36	1.25‡	.44[a]	10.05	
Canadian, ex Hamilton		7.65		.11[b]	7.76	2.29
Canadian, ex Sault Ste. Marie		7.50		.50[b]	8.00	2.05
Canadian, ex Sault Ste. Marie		7.50		.37[c]	7.87	2.18

Source: Compiled by The Algoma Steel Corporation, Limited, in Aug. 1967, and updated for a $5-per-ton increase in the United States in cold-rolled sheets, effective Jan. 1968.
Notes: Price is comprised of base price plus applicable extras.
U.S. funds converted to Canadian funds at premium rate of 7½%.
[a]Rail rate: 140,000 pounds minimum.
[b]Truck rate.
[c]Rail rate: 70,000 pounds minimum.
*Comparison with Buffalo, New York.
†Comparison with Pittsburgh, Pennsylvania.
‡Old tariff rates.

TABLE 20

COMPARISON OF CANADIAN AND U.S. LAID-DOWN PRICES OF SELECTED STEEL PRODUCTS AT MONTREAL AS OF AUGUST, 1967

(dollars per hundred pounds)

	Price		Duty	Freight to Montreal	Laid-down price	Canadian-U.S. laid-down price differential (amount by which Canadian laid-down price is lower)
	U.S. funds	Canadian funds				
Bars, carbon, hot-rolled						
2 × 2 × 1/4" angles—mild steel:						
U.S., ex Buffalo	6.83	7.34	.73	.86[a]	8.93	
Canadian, ex Hamilton		6.60		.42[b]	7.02	1.91
Canadian, ex Sault Ste. Marie		6.60		.55[b]	7.15	1.78
Canadian, ex Montreal		6.60			6.60	2.33
Light structurals						
4 × 4 × 5/16" angles—mild steel:						
U.S., ex Buffalo	6.55	7.04	.70	.86[a]	8.60	
U.S., ex Pittsburgh	6.55	7.04	.70	1.28[a]	9.02	
Canadian, ex Hamilton		6.25		.42[b]	6.67	1.93* / 2.35†
Canadian, ex Sault Ste. Marie		6.55		.55[b]	7.10	1.50* / 1.92†
Canadian, ex Montreal		6.25			6.25	2.35* / 2.77†
Heavy structurals						
12" × 27# WF-ASTM A-7:						
U.S., ex Buffalo	6.45	6.93	.69	.86[a]	8.48	
U.S., ex Pittsburgh	6.45	6.93	.69	1.28[a]	8.90	
Canadian, ex Sault Ste. Marie		6.45		.55[b]	7.00	1.48* / 1.90†
Plate, carbon						
72 × 3/8 × 240"—mild steel						
U.S., ex Pittsburgh	6.10	6.56	.66	1.28[a]	8.50	
Canadian, ex Hamilton		5.90		.42[b]	6.32	2.18
Canadian, ex Sault Ste. Marie		5.90		.55[b]	6.45	2.05
Plate for agricultural implements						
14 × 5/16 × 120" U.M. Plate SAE 1025:						
U.S., ex Pittsburgh	7.05	7.58	free	1.28[a]	8.86	
Canadian, ex Hamilton		6.95		.42[b]	7.37	1.49
Canadian, ex Sault Ste. Marie		6.95		.55[b]	7.50	1.36

TABLE 20 (continued)

	Price		Duty	Freight to Montreal	Laid-down price	Canadian-U.S. laid-down price differential (amount by which Canadian laid-down price is lower)
	U.S. funds	Canadian funds				
Sheets, hot-rolled						
48 × .1345″ × 240″—comm. qual.:						
U.S., ex Buffalo	6.40	6.88	.69	.86a	8.43	
Canadian, ex Hamilton		6.30		.42b	6.72	1.71
Canadian, ex Sault Ste. Marie		6.15		.55b	6.70	1.73
Canadian, ex Montreal		6.60			6.60	1.83
Sheets, cold-rolled						
48 × .0209″ × coil—comm. qual.:						
U.S., ex Buffalo	7.78	8.36	1.25‡	.86a	10.47	
Canadian, ex Hamilton		7.65		.42b	8.07	2.40
Canadian, ex Sault Ste. Marie		7.50		.55b	8.05	2.42
Canadian, ex Montreal		7.95			7.95	2.52

Source: See Table 19.
Notes: Price is comprised of base price plus applicable extras. U.S. funds converted to Canadian at premium rate of 7½%.
a The figures shown for U.S. shipment points are estimated as follows:
Freight ex Buffalo:
Buffalo-Hamilton $0.415 U.S. 40,000 lbs. minimum + 5% exchange surcharge = $0.435 Cdn.
Hamilton-Montreal   120,000 lbs. minimum   = 0.42 Cdn.
                                                         $0.855 Cdn.

Freight ex Pittsburgh:
Pittsburgh-Montreal $1.22 U.S. 40,000 lbs. minimum + 5% exchange surcharge = $1.28 Cdn.
Rail rate: 120,000 minimum lbs. for Hamilton and Sault Ste. Marie shipments.
*Comparison with Buffalo, New York.
†Comparison with Pittsburgh, Pennsylvania.
‡Old tariff rate.

TABLE 21

COMPARISON OF CANADIAN AND U.S. LAID-DOWN PRICES OF SELECTED STEEL PRODUCTS AT VANCOUVER AS OF AUGUST, 1967

(dollars per hundred pounds)

	Price		Duty	Freight to Vancouver	Laid-down price	Canadian-U.S. laid-down price differential (amount by which Canadian laid-down price is lower)
	U.S. funds	Canadian funds				
Bars, carbon, hot-rolled						
2 × 2 × 1/4″ angles—mild steel:						
U.S., ex Seattle	6.93	7.45	.74	.29[b]	8.48	
Canadian, ex Hamilton		6.60		1.27	7.87	.61
Canadian, ex Sault Ste. Marie		6.60		1.27	7.87	.61
Light structurals						
4 × 4 × 5/16″ angles—mild steel:						
U.S., ex Seattle	6.65	7.15	.71	.29[b]	8.15	
Canadian, ex Hamilton		6.25		1.27	7.52	.63
Canadian, ex Sault Ste. Marie		6.55		1.27	7.82	.33
Heavy structurals						
12″ × 27# WF—ASTM A-7:						
U.S., ex Minnequa	6.55	7.04	.70	1.41[b]	9.15	
Canadian, ex Sault Ste. Marie		6.45		1.16	7.61	1.54
Plate, carbon						
72 × 3/8 × 240″—mild steel:						
U.S., ex Geneva	6.10	6.56	.66	1.19[b]	8.41	
Canadian, ex Hamilton		5.90		1.27	7.17	1.24
Canadian, ex Sault Ste. Marie		5.90		1.27	7.17	1.24

TABLE 21 (continued)

	Price					Canadian-U.S. laid-down price differential (amounts by which Canadian laid down price is lower)
	U.S. funds	Canadian funds	duty	Freight to Vancouver	Laid-down price	
Sheet, hot-rolled						
60 × .1345 × 240''—comm. qual.:						
U.S., ex Geneva	6.55	7.04	.70	1.19[b]	8.93	
Canadian, ex Hamilton		6.35		1.27	7.62	1.31
Canadian, ex Sault Ste. Marie		6.20		1.27	7.47	1.46
Sheet, cold-rolled						
48 × .0299 × 120''—comm. qual.:						
U.S., ex Pittsburg, Calif.	7.78	8.36	1.25*	1.09[b]	10.70	
Canadian, ex Hamilton		7.65		1.27	8.92	1.78
Canadian, ex Sault Ste. Marie		7.50		1.27	8.77	1.93

Source: See Table 19.
Notes: Price is comprised of base price plus applicable extras. U.S. funds converted to Canadian funds at premium rate of $7\frac{1}{2}\%$.
[a] Rail rates, 80,000 lbs. minimum for U.S. mills and 140,000 lbs. minimum for Canadian mills except wide flange, which is 120,000 lbs. minimum for shipments from Sault Ste. Marie.
[b] The figures shown for U.S. shipment points are as follows:

Seattle-Vancouver $0.275 U.S. + 5% exchange surcharge = $0.29 Cdn.
Minnequa-Vancouver $1.34 U.S. + 5% exchange surcharge = $1.41 Cdn.
Geneva-Vancouver $1.13 U.S. + 5% exchange surcharge = $1.19 Cdn.
Pittsburg, Calif.-Vancouver $1.04 U.S. + 5% exchange surcharge = $1.09 Cdn.
*Old tariff rate.

Utah, are geographically much closer to Vancouver than the nearest integrated Canadian mill at Sault Ste. Marie, the structure of railroad freight rates still leaves the eastern mills (Hamilton, Montreal, and Sault Ste. Marie have identical rail rates) in a position of having only minor freight-cost disadvantages, amounting to $1.60 per ton compared with Geneva and $3.60 per ton compared with Fontana. Bars are available from a smaller plant at Seattle, Washington, which has a considerable freight-cost advantage.

However, on the west coast, the main origin of imported steel is not American, but Japanese, steel, which has a freight-cost advantage on ocean-going vessels in an extensive two-way freight trade by comparison to the Canadian overland rail rate.

The above dimensions of price—incorporating base prices plus extras (i.e., net prices), the exchange rate, the tariff duty on imported steel, and freight costs—are brought together in Tables 19 to 21, showing the competitive position of Canadian and U.S. steel at Toronto, Montreal, and Vancouver. The figures show the full differentials in laid-down prices that will have to be absorbed by mills competing at a particular delivery point. For example, Toronto steelbuyers, under normal conditions, would not pay more than the Hamilton base price, plus the $2.20-per-ton freight cost from Hamilton to Toronto.

The differences in laid-down theoretical prices are summarized in Table 22 below, showing the ratio of the Canadian to the U.S. prices at Toronto, Montreal, and Vancouver in January, 1968. In Toronto and Montreal the range by which Canadian prices are lower is from 14 percent to 26 percent for the specific products selected among the major categories of rolling mill products; except for heavy structurals, the differences cluster between 20 and 23 percent. At Vancouver, where the freight-cost advantages enjoyed by the Canadian mills in Toronto and Montreal are eliminated, the margin by which Canadian laid-down prices are lower is reduced—to 7 percent for the specific bar product (because it can be supplied from Seattle, Washington) and to between 15 and 17 percent in the four other products.

These figures emphasize the deterioration in the competitive position of U.S. steel in Canadian steel markets—a trend that has been documented in more elaborate statistical studies comparing the competitive position of U.S. steel relative to that of offshore suppliers. The National Bureau of Economic Research studies on the measurements of price change and international price competitiveness report the following conclusions to date with respect to iron and steel:

In 1964, international price levels of the United Kingdom and the EEC countries were below those of the U.S. for every one of the four groups. The U.S. price position was most unfavourable for iron and steel products. . . . The summary

TABLE 22

RATIO OF CANADIAN TO U.S. THEORETICAL LAID-DOWN STEEL PRICES, SELECTED DESTINATIONS AND PRODUCTS, AUGUST, 1967

Steel Production Points	Toronto		Montreal			Vancouver		
	Hamilton-Buffalo	Sault Ste Marie-Buffalo	Dosco, Montreal-Buffalo	Hamilton-Buffalo	Sault Ste Marie-Buffalo	Hamilton-Seattle	Sault Ste Marie-Minnequa	Hamilton-Geneva
Bars, carbon, hot-rolled 2 × 2 × 1/4" angles—mild steel	78.8		73.9	78.6		92.8		85.3
Heavy structurals 12' × 27# WF—ASTM A-7		86.2			82.5		83.2	
Plate, carbon 72 × 3/8 × 240"—mild steel	74.9††			74.4††				
Sheets, hot-rolled 60 × .1345 × 240"—commercial quality	80.1		78.3	79.7				85.3†
Sheets, cold-rolled* 48 × .0299 × 120"—commercial quality	77.2		75.9	77.1				83.4†

Source: Tables 19, 20 and 21.
*Based on old tariff rate of 15 percent.
†The ratios based on a Sault Ste. Marie-Geneva comparison would be slightly lower, as the Sault base prices are $3 per ton lower, and the freight rates from Hamilton and the Sault to Vancouver are identical.
††Hamilton-Pittsburgh.

indexes conceal a good deal of variability in subgroup price ratios and, of course, more in the ratios for individual products. However, the ratios do cluster around the averages shown, with the greatest number of subgroups of iron and steel, for example, and those with the greatest value of trade, showing U.K. and EEC price ratios between 80 and 85 per cent of U.S. prices. Japanese indexes for iron and steel [not shown in Table 23 below] point to a price level considerably below the European one, at about 25–30 percent beneath the U.S. price level.

TABLE 23

COMPARATIVE INTERNATIONAL PRICE LEVELS,
1964, IRON AND STEEL, SITC 67
(United States = 100)

United States	100
United Kingdom	81
European Coal and Steel Community	80
West Germany	81

Source: Irving B. Kravis and R. E. Lipsey, "The Measurement of Price Change: A Report on the Study of International Price Competitiveness", *American Economic Review*, Vol. LVII, no. 2, May 1967, p. 485.

On the matter of changes in price competitiveness, Kravis and Lipsey found that:

The largest changes in international price competitiveness, that is, the relationship of foreign prices to U.S. prices of internationally traded goods, have taken place in iron and steel. Mostly these have been unfavourable to the United States, with a decline of almost 20 per cent in U.S. price competitiveness relative to the European countries between 1953 and 1963 [Table 24]. In 1964, however, there was a reversal of the trend, with U.S. price competitiveness rebounding to better levels than in any of the three preceding years. Relative to Japan there was a decline in U.S. price competitiveness between 1961 and 1962 and no change after that. Despite the gain in 1964, however, the position of the United States in iron and steel remained considerably worse than in 1953 and 1957.[50]

A broader assessment of changes in international price competitiveness is reserved for chapter 3, when we will be considering trends among the U.S. and major steel producers outside North America. Given published base prices and reasonably accurate measurements for transportation costs, the documentation of Canadian and U.S. steel-price trends is generally workable and valid. In turning to offshore comparisons, both concepts and measure-

[50]Kravis and Lipsey, p. 486.

TABLE 24

INDEXES OF U.S. PRICE COMPETITIVENESS[a] RELATIVE TO THAT OF THE
UNITED KINGDOM, GERMANY, THE EEC, AND JAPAN, 1953–64
(1962 = 100)

	1953	1957	1961	1962	1963	1964
SITC 67 Iron and steel						
Relative to United Kingdom	120	110	101	100	97	103
Relative to EEC	121	119	103	100	98	105
Relative to Germany	115	112	103	100	96	104
Relative to Japan	n.a.	n.a.	108	100	100	100

Source: Irving B. Kravis and R. E. Lipsey, "The Measurement of Price Change," p. 487.
Note: The indexes are averages of indexes for smaller groups on the three-, four-, or
five-digit SITC level, weighted for the importance of each subgroup in world trade.
Estimates are included for most three-digit components and are subject to some revision.
[a]These indexes show the relationship between the change in foreign prices and the
change in U.S. prices. For example, the figure of 103 for SITC 67 relative to the United
Kingdom in 1964 shows that U.K. prices have risen 3 percent more than U.S. prices
since the 1962 base year or, if derived from price-level data, that the ratio of the U.K.
price level to the U.S. price level was 3 percent higher in 1964 than in the base year 1962.

ments become more difficult because most offshore steel exporters use "two-
price" systems, differentiating home market prices from export prices.

Secondly, ocean freight cost information is sporadic and does not have
the same statistical precision as do overland movements in Canada and the
United States by rail or by truck. Since freight costs are a relatively high
proportion of the total delivered price of steel, the area of imprecision in
international comparisons of transport costs is a stumbling block to accurate
assessments of relative competitiveness of offshore, compared with Canadian,
steel. Of these two issues, the two-price system, of course, raises the greatest
complications for our analysis, particularly because of its important implications for anti-dumping policy (see pages 105–8).

To conclude the subject of Canadian steel-price trends, it is clear that on
the evidence of the specific measurements made, Canadian steel prices have
declined significantly relative to those in the United States, from a prewar
situation where Canadian steel prices were significantly higher than those in
the United States to current conditions where there is a significant margin
in the other direction. Combined with the rapid expansion of productive
facilities by the Canadian industry, the displacement of imports—particularly
those from the United States—becomes a major trend in Canadian steel
markets, to a point where the present position of U.S. steel in Canadian
markets is limited to those few products that are still not being supplied by
the Canadian industry because of an insufficiency of demand in relation to the

TABLE 25

FINANCIAL RATIOS OF SELECTED MAJOR ATLANTIC STEEL INDUSTRIES, 1960–65

Country	Number of companies	1960	1961	1962	1963	1964	1965
		| Profits after taxes—total assets (percent)					
Belgium	8	4.3	4.8	4.3	1.3	1.3	.5
Luxembourg	3	5.4	3.1	3.1	(.2)	1.6	4.9
Netherlands	2,3	11.6	8.6	6.2	5.8	5.8	4.7
Germany	17	4.7	4.5	2.0	1.7 (2)	2.4 (2)	1.5 (2)
France	14,15 (14)	1.0	1.4	.9	1.5	.5	.3
Italy	7	3.1	3.3	5.4	2.5	3.4	1.0
United Kingdom	15	10.0	5.3	2.4	1.9	1.7	
Japan	6	2.8	3.1	1.4	2.7	2.8	2.0
United States	33	5.1	4.1	3.5	4.6	5.3	
Canada	4		6.7	7.0	7.8	7.4	6.5
		| Profits after taxes—equity (percent)					
Belgium	8	8.1	8.8	8.3	2.7	2.8	1.0
Luxembourg	3	8.3	4.7	4.7	(.2)	2.3	7.4
Netherlands	2,3	15.1	10.9	7.9	7.3	7.2	5.9
Germany	17	9.7	9.5	4.4	3.9 (2)	5.8 (2)	3.7 (2)
France	14,15 (14)	2.4	3.6	2.5	4.2	1.4	.8
Italy	7	7.6	8.3	12.1	7.1	10.9	3.7
United Kingdom	15	15.6	8.7	4.1	3.5	3.1	
Japan	6	8.1	9.5	4.3	8.5	8.6	6.6
United States	33	7.6	6.2	5.2	6.9	8.0	
Canada	4		9.9	10.4	11.1	11.7	11.0

TABLE 25 (continued)

Country	Number of companies	1960	1961	1962	1963	1964	1965
				Profits after taxes—total revenue (percent)			
Belgium	3, 4, 5	4.4	6.0	5.8	(4) 1.6	(5) 0.8	(5) (0.1)
Luxembourg	1, 2	(1) 19.3	3.1	3.8	(1.1)	3.1	(2) 6.1
Netherlands	17	3.7	15.4	14.1	10.3	(1) 11.1	(1) 10.8
Germany	14, 15	.7	3.7	1.7	1.6	2.1	1.3
France	7		1.4	1.0	(14) 2.1	(14) .5	.4
Italy		4.4	5.0	9.3	5.7	10.9	2.9
United Kingdom	2, 6	(2) 13.8	(2) 9.7	2.8	2.7	1.1	
Japan	6	4.0	4.7	2.7	4.7	4.5	3.2
United States	33	6.0	5.3	4.3	5.6	6.0	
Canada	4			8.6	9.6	9.0	8.4
				Profits after taxes—steel ingots produced (dollars per short ton)			
Belgium	8	4.51	5.60	5.19	2.79	2.52	0.91
Luxembourg	3	4.58	2.87	3.02	(.17)	1.49	4.95
Netherlands	2, 3	20.00	16.74	13.71	12.33	15.62	(2) 11.61
Germany	17	6.79	7.42	3.63	3.38	4.34	2.55
France	14, 15	(14) 1.14	2.06	1.54	3.02	.87	.46
Italy	7	6.19	6.91	12.99	7.93	15.23	3.16
United Kingdom	15	16.08	9.99	5.49	4.48	3.53	
Japan	6	4.55	5.19	2.87	4.93	4.65	3.33
United States	33	8.72	7.91	6.22	7.60	7.98	
Canada	3		11.55	10.94	11.56	11.93	11.38

Sources: Canada: compiled from annual reports of companies. Other countries: *Steel Import Study*, p. 448.
Note: The percentages of total ingot output accounted for by the companies shown for individual countries in 1964 were:

Belgium, Luxembourg, Netherlands, United States, and Canada	90–100 percent
West Germany, France, and the United Kingdom	80–89 percent
Japan	79 percent
Italy	61 percent

minimum economic scale of production, or because of a short supply in relation to peak cyclical demands (e.g., 1965).

G. FINANCIAL COMPARISONS

The recent compilation and publication of financial data for U.S. and major non-Communist steel producers make it possible to obtain comparative financial trends in the Atlantic nations' steel industries.[51]

Table 25 shows the data published in the U.S. Senate *Steel Import Study*, with comparable figures for the Canadian industry. The first two comparisons are in key financial ratios, showing profits after taxes as a ratio of total assets and total shareholders' equity. A country-by-country ranking based on 1962 to 1965 arithmetic averages appears in Table 26; this puts the Canadian group at the top of the list in each of the two ratios, followed in second place by the Netherlands in terms of the return on total assets and by Italy on the basis of the return on total shareholders' equity. The U.S. industry ranks third in return on total assets and fifth on total shareholders' equity; Japan's ranking is, respectively, sixth and fourth. The large ECSC steel industries— in West Germany, France, Belgium—are at the bottom of the list in terms of the rate of return on assets; Luxembourg and the United Kingdom are in the middle of the range.

The two other comparisons are profits after taxes as a percentage of sales and per ton of crude steel produced. Both of these are more general indicators of financial performance and also are partly proxy measures of the depth of vertical integration. Here the Dutch performance tops the list, followed in order by Canada, Italy, and the United States. The other nations' returns are significantly lower and approximately in the same ranking order as appears on the basis of the first two criteria.

A number of interesting hypotheses arise from the financial data. The relatively small steel industry in the Netherlands—its rated raw steel capacity in 1966 was only 3.8 million net tons, or 3.2 percent of the 119.7-million-ton ECSC total—shows a financial position distinct from the larger ECSC producers. The apparent reasons for this are a very rapid growth in industrial production and metal-fabricating industries in the last decade and a sharp expansion of the domestic steel industry (from a capacity of 1.2 million net

[51]For the U.S. and the other major countries' data, see U.S. Senate, *Steel Import Study*, pp. 437–59. The data were prepared for the Senate Finance Committee by the Business and Defense Services Administration of the U.S. Department of Commerce and included financial statements of more than one hundred companies, using the procedures of the ECSC's Goudima reports. The Canadian data combine financial statements of Stelco, Algoma, Dofasco, and Dosco. It should be kept in mind that international comparisons of this type present more than the usual conceptual accounting and statistical difficulties —the results shown here should be interpreted in the light of such reservations.

51 CANADIAN IRON AND STEEL INDUSTRY

TABLE 26

PROFITABILITY RATIOS OF SELECTED ATLANTIC NATIONS' STEEL INDUSTRIES, 1962–65
(arithmetic averages)

	Ratio of profits after taxes to total assets	Ratio of profits after taxes to total shareholders' equity	Ratio of profits after taxes to total revenue	Profits after taxes per short ton of crude steel (U.S. $/short ton)
Canada	7.2	11.1	8.9	11.45
Netherlands	5.6	7.1	11.6	13.32
United States[a]	4.5	6.7	5.3	7.27
Italy	3.1	8.5	7.2	9.83
Luxembourg	2.4	3.4	3.0	2.32
Japan	2.2	7.0	3.8	3.95
United Kingdom[a]	2.0	3.6	2.2	4.50
West Germany	1.9	4.5	1.7	3.48
Belgium	1.9	3.7	2.0	2.85
France	0.8	2.2	1.0	1.47

Source: Compiled from Table 25. The rankings are in descending order on the basis of rate of return on total assets.
[a]1962 to 1964.

TABLE 27

RATIOS OF DEBT TO EQUITY CAPITAL EMPLOYED AND
INTEREST COSTS TO TOTAL REVENUE,
SELECTED ATLANTIC NATIONS' STEEL INDUSTRIES, 1964

	Ratio of debt to equity	Ratio of interest costs to total revenue
Italy	142.4	3.3
France	130.4	3.0
Japan	128.4	5.3
West Germany	103.7	1.7
Belgium	80.5	3.4
United States	17.3	0.8
United Kingdom	16.4	2.0
Canada	16.0	0.5
Netherlands	13.3	1.0[a]
Luxembourg	10.3	0.7[a]

Sources: Canada: Compiled from annual reports of companies. Other countries: *Steel Import Study*, pp. 449 and 452.
Note: Coverage same as shown in Table 25.
[a]1965; 1964 not available.

tons in 1956), enabling it to reduce its relative dependence on imported steel and to build up substantial export volumes to ECSC and third countries (particularly in flat-rolled products). In addition, virtually the entire output of the country is concentrated in a single company, the Koninglijke Neder-landsche Hoogovens en Staalfabrieken, N.V.

The Italian performance ranks next best in the ECSC. Again this repre-sents an industry still in a takeoff period, growing from 7.2 million net tons of capacity in 1956 to 19.1 million net tons in 1966, and maintaining operating ratios generally high by comparison with those of other members of the Community, with the exception of Luxembourg. The Italian industry also appears to have benefited substantially from domestic conditions propi-tious for economic growth. The rise in total industrial production has been the sharpest in the European Economic Community, as has per capita steel consumption, though, of course, in terms of levels, Italy started below those of the EEC. In foreign trade, Italy has built a net export position in relation to third countries (largely in structurals and sheets), but it (as well as the Netherlands) remains a net importer in intra-ECSC trade.

Another aspect of financial structure which is relevant to later areas in this study is the capital structure of the various nations' steel industries, and particularly the extent to which debt capital is relied upon. Table 27 shows the 1964 ratios of debt to equity capital and interest costs to total revenue. The figures emphasize the extent to which debt capital (and the fixed interest charges attending its use) plays a significantly larger role in the capital structure of most of the ECSC members[52] and Japan, particularly by comparison with the United States and Canada.

[52]With the exception of Luxembourg and the Netherlands.

2. Postwar Developments in the Atlantic Nations' Steel Industries and the Current State of International Steel Trade

Introduction

We now turn to an analysis of trends in the steel industries of the Atlantic nations. These provide the second set of building blocks necessary for an evaluation of the alternatives in the Atlantic Economic Studies Program.

This chapter sketches briefly the postwar trends in these steel industries and relates them to the emerging international steel-trade situation. This will be done in detail for the United States, the ECSC as a group, Japan, the United Kingdom, and the other EFTA members. In addition, this chapter includes a detailed analysis of the Canadian steel trade (summarized in chapter 1).

Following this analysis of industry trends and of the structure of steel trade among the Atlantic nations, we turn our attention to important commercial-policy issues in the international steel trade. These include the price policies of offshore producers, tariff changes, and aspects of non-tariff commercial policy, with emphasis on the new anti-dumping agreement reached at the Kennedy round–GATT negotiations.

From the many studies on the international steel situation and from the maze of statistics available, the following facts on world steel trends emerge:
1. At the end of World War II, the world steel situation was characterized by
   (a) a shortage of steel supplies in many parts of the world, resulting from heavy destruction of the industries in a number of the important producing countries and from the requirements of reconstruction.
   (b) the powerful position of the U.S. steel industry, whose output accounted for 55 percent of the world's total in the immediate postwar years.
   (c) a desire on the part of the Europeans and the Japanese to rebuild their war-torn economies, and the requirements this imposed for rebuilding and expanding their steel industries.
2. From a condition of general excess demand for steel in relation to available supplies in the first decade after World War II, the rapid growth of the

steel industries in the major producing nations gave rise to a better balance between supply and demand by the mid-1950s.

3. In the late 1950s, increases in the capacity to produce steel began to outrun the gains in demand, thus creating an excess of potential supply. The excess capacity was initially located in the United States but has since then spread to most of the other major producers in the Atlantic nations group. This change reflects the following developments:

(a) A rate of expansion in productive capacity, particularly within the ECSC, which has proven to be significantly ahead of the requirements of domestic demand, or any probable export opportunities.

(b) The gains in steel production in the smaller industrial countries, which heretofore had relied to an important degree on imported steel. Modern and competitive steel industries, generally capable of competing with the imports of the traditional world exporters, have been established in Canada, Australia, and South Africa. In addition, many smaller countries have erected steel industries of their own which, though less efficient, are often insulated from imports by restrictive domestic commercial policies.

(c) A number of countries in the eastern European Communist bloc (which have also experienced a rapid rise in productive capacity available) have entered the steel markets of the Atlantic nations. The competition from the Communist bloc, which cannot be placed in the same analytical framework as the international trade of those countries relying largely on prices as a market mechanism, has, at times, disrupted the ECSC market.

Over-all, steel has moved from an initial postwar market condition of shortages and low levels of international trade to a situation where a significant amount of unused steel capacity hangs heavy over the international trade picture. This change can be illustrated by summary statistics on world steel capacity, output, and trade.

The two sets of figures shown in Table 28 are for the world and the world excluding the Communist bloc. Both because of the less precise meaning of its capacity-production relationships and because it falls outside our Atlantic nations reference, our subsequent analysis is in terms of the non-Communist world, even though steel trade with the bloc is in some instances taken into account.

The data in Table 28 highlight the sharp surges in capacity and production during the postwar period and also emphasize the gradual buildup of excess production capacity. At first the excess capacity was concentrated in the United States. For example, the ratio of output to capacity in 1960 in the

TABLE 28

WORLD STEEL CAPACITY, PRODUCTION, AND INTERNATIONAL TRADE,
SELECTED YEARS, 1937–65, AND 1970 FORECAST
(Volume figures in millions of tons of raw steel)

	Capacity	Production	Ratio of production to capacity	Excess capacity	International trade in steel	
					Exports (or imports)	Percentage of production
1937	192.1	149.5	78	42.6	21.5	14
1950	217.7	207.1	95	10.6	23.6	11
1957	363.4	321.7	89	41.7	45.8	14
1960	446.9	381.6	85	65.3	58.3	15
1965	568.2	503.1	89	65.1	88.6	18
1970	748.0	647.0	86	101.0		
Excluding Communist bloc						
1937	164.4	124.3	76	40.1	20.4	16
1950	177.7	168.6	95	9.1	22.0	13
1957	282.8	242.0	86	40.8	40.7	17
1960	330.4	265.7	80	64.7	51.4	19
1965	421.7	357.1	85	64.6	74.4	21
1970	537.0	437.0	82	100.0		

Sources: 1937 to 1965: U.S. Senate, *Steel Import Study*, p. 269, and data compiled from ECE, AISI, and the British Iron and Steel Federation. 1970 forecast: OECD.

non-Communist countries, excluding the United States, was a relatively high 92 percent, compared to only 80 percent if the United States is included. Since then the excess capacity has become more widespread. It was estimated at 65 million net tons in 1965—15 percent of total capacity—and the most recent projections of the Special Committee for Iron and Steel of the OECD, based on current expansion plans and projections of world demand, put the amount of excess capacity in the non-Communist world at 100 million tons and 18 percent by 1970.

This figure is a focal point on the current world steel scene. It lurks in the background of the commercial-policy deliberations of the day—at the GATT, before the United States Congress, and at the recent first International Iron and Steel Institute meeting in Brussels. It is also important to our analysis in chapter 3, as the presence of large volumes of excess capacity, particularly among the export-oriented industries of the ECSC, has had a pervasive impact on the conditions of world steel trade and consequently affects our terms of reference.

Postwar trends in the steel industries of the Atlantic nations

Tables 29 and 30 to 35 summarize the important production trends and international trading relationships among the "Atlantic nations," as defined for the purposes of this study. The trade statistics, summarized for the years 1953, 1959, and 1965, are from the annual compilations of the ECE.[1]

A. UNITED STATES

At the end of World War II, the steel industry of the United States was in a dominant position, accounting for an average of almost 51 percent of total world production between the years 1947 to 1949, and 61 percent of the output of the non-Communist world (see Table 29). The catching-up on private demands postponed by World War II and the relatively rapid economic growth of the first postwar decade led to a large expansion of U.S. steel output, though this was intermittently interrupted by recessions in 1949 and 1954 and by a letup in demand during 1952 following the initial Korean War buildup. Output of raw steel, which averaged 84 million tons from 1947 to 1949, reached a peak of 117 million tons in 1955.

The second postwar decade shows up as a sharp contrast. The slow economic growth of the late 1950s, the recessions of 1957 to 1958 and 1960 to 1961, the steel strike of 1959, and the gradually rising volumes of imported steel resulted in a generally downward trend in output, with production falling below 100 million tons for five consecutive years from 1958 to 1962. The 1955 peak of 117 million tons was not exceeded again until output reached 127 million tons in 1964, and again in 1965 and 1966, when, under the impetus of a major boom in capital-investment expenditures, output exceeded the 130-million-ton mark. In spite of the relatively sharp cyclical expansion of steel output in the 1960s, the U.S. industry has lost ground in comparison with trends in most of the world's major steel-producing nations. In the context of non-Communist world production, and more specifically in relation to the Atlantic nations group, this can be illustrated by the figures in Table 29.

For example, the ratio of U.S. to non-Communist world production declined from an average of 61 percent in 1947 to 1949 to 37 percent by 1966. In relation to the Atlantic nations group, for which details are shown in

[1]The products included in these tables are those covered by the ECSC treaty. They are ingots and semi-finished steel and all steel rolling mill products. Excluded are steel tubes and fittings, wire, and other products of a more advanced stage of manufacture than rolling mill products. International trade data for manufactured products are readily available in the ECE's annual compilations, the Statistical Office of the European Communities, and the trade statistics of individual countries. They are specifically omitted from consideration in this survey.

TABLE 29

RAW STEEL PRODUCTION, NON-COMMUNIST WORLD AND THE ATLANTIC NATIONS, 1947–49 AVERAGE, 1955, 1960, AND 1966

	Millions of net tons				Percentage of total				Output index 1947–49 average = 100		
	1947–49 average	1955	1960	1966	1947–49 average	1955	1960	1966	1955	1960	1966
Non-Communist world total	137.8	228.7	265.7	365.3	100.0	100.0	100.0	100.0	166	193	265
United States	83.8	117.0	99.3	134.1	60.8	51.2	37.4	36.7	140	118	160
ECSC	25.5	58.0	80.3	93.8	18.5	25.4	30.2	25.7	227	315	368
Japan	2.1	10.4	24.4	52.7	1.5	4.5	9.2	14.4	495	1,162	2,510
United Kingdom	15.7	22.2	27.2	27.2	11.4	9.7	10.2	7.4	141	173	173
Other EFTA	2.3	5.0	8.2	10.7	1.7	2.2	3.1	2.9	217	357	465
Canada	3.1	4.5	5.8	10.0	2.2	2.0	2.2	2.7	145	187	323
Total Atlantic	132.5	217.1	245.2	328.5	96.2	94.9	92.3	89.9	164	185	248
All other	5.3	11.6	20.5	36.8	3.8	5.1	7.7	10.1	219	387	694

Source: Compiled from U.S. Senate, *Steel Import Study*, pp. 256–61.
Note: Details may not add to totals because of rounding.

TABLES 30-32

WORLD TRADE IN STEEL ROLLING MILL PRODUCTS, 1953, 1959, AND 1965

(thousands of net tons)

30. 1953

Imported into		Exported from							
	ECSC	United States	Japan	United Kingdom	Other EFTA	Canada	Subtotal, Atlantic group	Rest of world	Total
ECSC	2,901	223	65	207	208	1	3,605	11	3,616
United States	1,108	—	26	69	19	184	1,406	—	1,406
Japan	17	41	—	6	6	4	74	6	80
United Kingdom	556	85	51	—	115	33	840	76	916
Other EFTA	1,333	139	—	265	116	—	1,853	6	1,859
Canada	110	840	4	121	1	—	1,076	—	1,076
Subtotal, Atlantic group	6,025	1,328	146	668	465	222	8,854	99	8,953
Rest of world	3,810	1,079	631	931	101	198	6,750	13,401	20,151
Total	9,835	2,407	777	1,599	566	420	15,604	13,500	29,104

31. 1959

Imported into		Exported from							
	ECSC	United States	Japan	United Kingdom	Other EFTA	Canada	Subtotal, Atlantic group	Rest of world	Total
ECSC	7,339	141	—	200	649	3	8,332	211	8,543
United States	2,173	—	402	116	69	317	3,077	1	3,078
Japan	44	57	—	173	1	1	276	4	280
United Kingdom	310	31	—	—	23	—	364	19	383
Other EFTA	2,395	46	7	327	254	1	3,030	134	3,164
Canada	233	510	44	152	1	—	940	—	940
Subtotal, Atlantic group	12,494	785	453	968	997	322	16,019	369	16,388
Rest of world	6,659	642	940	1,269	599	67	10,176	3,796	13,972
Total	19,153	1,427	1,393	2,237	1,596	389	26,195	4,165	30,360

32. 1965

Imported into	Exported from								
	ECSC	United States	Japan	United Kingdom	Other EFTA	Canada	Subtotal, Atlantic group	Rest of world	Total
ECSC	12,975	84	172	445	1,011	8	14,695	536	15,231
United States	3,759	—	3,628	646	85	595	8,713	89	8,802
Japan	3	7	—	—	—	—	10	34	44
United Kingdom	357	12	6	—	164	8	547	109	656
Other EFTA	3,830	26	15	509	608	2	4,990	290	5,280
Canada	904	525	194	190	11	—	1,824	37	1,861
Subtotal, Atlantic group	21,828	654	4,015	1,790	1,879	613	30,779	1,095	31,874
Rest of world	7,606	1,479	4,713	1,833	642	246	16,519	8,815	25,334
Total	29,434	2,133	8,728	3,623	2,521	859	47,298	9,910	57,208

Source: Compiled from United Nations, ECE, *Statistics of World Trade in Steel.*

TABLES 33–34

PERCENTAGE DISTRIBUTION OF ATLANTIC NATIONS' STEEL TRADE, 1953 AND 1965

33. 1953

			Exported from				
Imported into	ECSC	United States	Japan	United Kingdom	Other EFTA	Canada	Total, Atlantic group
ECSC	32.8	2.5	0.7	2.3	2.4	a	40.7
United States	12.5	—	0.3	0.8	0.2	2.1	15.9
Japan	0.2	0.5	—	a	a	a	0.8
United Kingdom	6.3	1.0	0.6	—	1.3	0.4	9.5
Other EFTA	15.1	1.5	—	3.0	1.3	—	20.9
Canada	1.2	9.5	a	1.4	a	—	12.1
Total	68.1	15.0	1.6	7.5	5.2	2.5	100.0

34. 1965

			Exported from				
Imported into	ECSC	United States	Japan	United Kingdom	Other EFTA	Canada	Total, Atlantic group
ECSC	42.2	0.3	0.6	1.4	3.3	a	47.7
United States	12.2	—	11.8	2.1	0.3	1.9	28.3
Japan	a	a	—	—	—	a	a
United Kingdom	1.2	a	a	—	0.5	a	1.8
Other EFTA	12.4	0.1	0.1	1.7	2.0	a	16.2
Canada	2.9	1.7	0.6	0.6	a	—	5.9
Total	70.9	2.1	13.1	5.8	6.1	1.9	100.0

Source: Tables 30 and 32.
Note: Details may not add to totals because of rounding.
aLess than 0.1 percent.

Table 29 and which accounts for some 90 percent of all non-Communist world production, the decline in the share of U.S. production was from 63 percent to 41 percent. A similar trend is mirrored by the production indexes appearing in Table 29; here the growth in U.S. output is 60 percent from a 1947 to 1949 base to 1966; this is smallest among the list of countries or groups of countries shown in the table.

The ratio of capacity utilization by the U.S. steel industry remained generally high in the first postwar decade, except in 1949, 1952, and 1954; but following the boom of the mid-1950s, it fell sharply, reaching 61 percent in 1958 and remaining below 65 percent in 1959. The official capacity compilations by the American Iron and Steel Institute were discontinued after 1960, but estimates of the U.S. capacity by the *Wall Street Journal* since then have shown that utilization remained under 70 percent from 1961 to 1963 and recovered to a range of 77 to 78 percent from 1964 to 1966.

TABLE 35

1965 INDEXES OF WORLD STEEL TRADE

(1953 = 100)

Imported into	ECSC	United States	Japan	United Kingdom	Other EFTA	Canada	Subtotal, Atlantic group	Rest of world	Total
						Exported from			
ECSC	447	38	264	215	485	[a]	408	4,872	421
United States	339	—	13,954	936	[a]	323	619	[a]	626
Japan	[a]	[a]	—	[a]	[a]	[a]	[a]	[a]	[a]
United Kingdom	64	19	[a]	—	143	[a]	65	143	72
Other EFTA	287	62	4,850	193	523	[a]	270	4,833	284
Canada	822	49	2,750	156	[a]	—	169	[a]	173
Subtotal, Atlantic group	362	137	748	268	405	275		1,106	356
Rest of world	200			197	636	124	348	66	126
Total	299	89	1,123	227	446	205		73	197

Source: Tables 30 and 32.

[a]No trade in base period, or trade less than 100,000 net tons in both years.

Although steel experts dispute the general validity of the unofficial capacity estimates, contending that some of the capacity counted is obsolete, the view remains that substantial excess capacity exists in the U.S. steel industry. On the basis of more conservative Economic Commission for Europe figures, which put U.S. capacity in 1965 at 156.5 million net tons (compared to the 168 million tons estimated by the *Wall Street Journal*), the excess capacity in that year would still have amounted to 25 million tons and 16 percent.

Historically the United States has been a net exporter of steel rolling mill products, although the volume of exports in relation to total production has generally not been a major factor in the industry's over-all operations. Both in 1929 and from 1936 to 1938, steel-product exports were just over 2 million tons, compared to imports amounting to less than 500,000 tons, leaving an export balance of about 2 million tons. These patterns continued after World War II; from 1950 to 1958, exports were in a range of from 3 to 5 million tons, and imports in a range of from 1 to 2 million tons, leaving a surplus in steel trade ranging from 1 to 4 million tons. The largest absolute surpluses on steel-products trade occurred between 1955 and 1957, when exports averaged 4.6 million tons, while imports were slightly more than 1 million tons, leaving a net export surplus of some 3.5 million tons per year.

The year 1958 marks a turning point in the U.S. international steel-trading position, as exports began to decline, while imports began a sharp and long rise. From a level ranging between 1 and 2 million tons in the mid-1950s, imports increased to a range of 3 to 4 million tons from 1959 to 1962. They exceeded 5 million tons in 1963 and were between 10 and 11½ million tons from 1965 to 1967. Combined with a gradual decline in exports, into a range generally between 2 and 3 million tons, the U.S. balance of trade in steel rolling mill products turned negative in 1959 (for that year, the explanation lies partly in the prolonged steel strike) and has been on the minus side every year since then. In the early 1960s the deficit was typically between 1 and 3 million tons, but by 1965 it had soared to 8 million tons, and it reached 9 million tons in 1966.

The ratio of imports to total apparent consumption of steel rolling mill products averaged 1.5 percent between 1955 and 1957, 5 percent between 1960 and 1962, and exceeded 10 percent in both 1965 and 1966. Similarly, exports, which had averaged about 5 percent of total mill shipments in the mid-1950s, subsequently fell to a level of around 2 percent in the mid-1960s. Additional statistics summarizing the U.S. output and steel-trade trends are shown in Table 36.

The turnabout in the U.S. international steel-trade position has been a major change in the world steel-trading picture of the last decade. The decline reflects the following changes in the world steel situation:

(a) A buildup of domestic production facilities in a number of countries
(such as Canada, Australia, and South Africa) which had heretofore been
net importers of steel. In the Canadian case, the impact on the U.S. trade
picture is particularly important, as American steel had historically been the
main source of supply (see Table 49).
(b) The rapid growth of the ECSC and Japanese steel industries. The combined output of the ECSC and Japan had been less than one-third of that of
the United States in the early postwar period, but the output by the 1960s
was actually larger than that of the United States. In the process, the ECSC
and the Japanese not only became competitors in such world markets as had
been previously served by U.S. steel, but also became gradually a more
significant source of supply to the U.S. market.
(c) As we have seen in relation to the Canadian price data (see pages 32–44
above), the competitive position of U.S. steel in international markets started
deteriorating during the 1950s, and clearly in the Canadian case this was a
major reason for the sharp displacement of U.S. steel in the Canadian
market.

As the data summarizing the geographical composition of steel trade
among the Atlantic nations show (see Tables 32 and 34), imports from the
ECSC and Japan account for the bulk of the U.S. total, followed by the
United Kingdom and Canada. By comparison, U.S. exports are mainly to
Canada and countries outside the Atlantic group, with the ECSC purchasing
token quantities and the Japanese purchasing amounts that are statistically
insignificant.[2] The growth of, and persistent trend in, imports have had a
profound impact on the attitude of the U.S. steel industry, and partly on the
U.S. government, in their commercial-policy stances. As we will see in our
analysis of the Kennedy round results, the major impact on steel of the
Kennedy round will probably come from the new anti-dumping agreement,
as most of the tariff-rate changes do not appear to be a factor that will
significantly increase the volume of trade among the developed nations. However, of much greater concern to the world trade picture has been the massive
campaign by the U.S. steel industry during 1967 to attempt to get more pro-
tectionist legislation from the United States Congress, either by means of a
higher temporary tariff or by quotas on steel imports.

B. THE EUROPEAN COAL AND STEEL COMMUNITY

The rebuilding of the severely damaged steel industries in continental Europe,
and their subsequent rise into the second largest steel complex in the world,
ranks as a significant landmark in the history of steel of the postwar era. Steel

[2]The proportion of exports financed under AID arrangements has also risen sharply,
from 4 percent of the value of steel exports in 1959 to 32 percent in 1966.

TABLE 36

STEEL INDUSTRY AND MARKET DATA, UNITED STATES, 1946–67
(volume figures in millions of net tons)

	Raw steel			Rolled steel products					
	Capacity	Output	Operating ratio	Total shipments	Imports	Exports	Apparent consumption*	Imports as a percentage of apparent consumption	Exports as a percentage of total shipments
1946	91.9	66.6	72.5						
1947	91.2	84.9	93.1	63.1					
1948	94.2	88.6	94.1	66.0					
1949	96.1	78.0	81.1	58.1					
1950	100.0	96.8	96.9	72.2	1.2	2.8	70.6	1.7	3.9
1951	104.2	105.1	100.9	78.9	2.3	3.2	78.0	2.9	4.1
1952	108.6	93.2	85.8	68.0	1.2	4.0	65.2	1.8	5.9
1953	117.5	111.6	94.9	80.2	1.6	3.1	78.7	2.0	3.9
1954	124.3	88.3	71.0	63.2	0.8	2.8	61.2	1.3	4.4
1955	125.8	117.0	93.0	84.7	1.0	4.1	81.6	1.2	4.8
1956	128.4	115.2	89.8	83.3	1.3	4.3	80.3	1.6	5.2
1957	133.5	112.7	84.5	79.9	1.2	5.3	75.8	1.6	6.6
1958	140.7	85.3	60.6	59.9	1.7	2.8	58.8	2.9	4.7
1959	147.6	93.4	63.3	69.4	4.4	1.7	72.1	6.1	2.4
1960	148.6	99.3	66.8	71.1	3.4	3.0	71.5	4.8	4.2
1961	150.0	98.0	65.3	66.1	3.2	2.0	67.3	4.8	3.0
1962	157.0	98.3	62.6	70.6	4.1	2.0	72.7	5.6	2.8
1963	162.0	109.3	67.5	75.6	5.5	2.2	78.9	7.0	2.9
1964	165.0	127.0	77.0	84.9	6.4	3.4	87.9	7.3	4.0
1965	168.0	131.5	78.3	92.7	10.4	2.5	100.6	10.3	2.7
1966	174.0	134.1	77.1	90.0	10.8	1.7	99.1	10.9	1.9
1967	183.0	127.2	69.5	83.9	11.5	1.7	93.7	12.2	2.0

Sources: American Iron and Steel Institute; U.S. Senate, *Steel Import Study*; and *American Metal Market*.
*Apparent consumption = total shipments + imports − exports.
Note: Computations made from unrounded data.

TABLE 37

STEEL INDUSTRY AND MARKET DATA, ECSC, 1946-67

(volume figures in millions of net tons)

	Raw steel			Steel consumption	Rolled steel products					
	Capacity	Output	Operating ratio	(raw steel)	Output	Imports (net)[a]	Exports (net)[a]	Apparent consumption[b]	Exports as a percentage of output	Imports as a percentage of apparent consumption
1946		14.1								
1947		19.0								
1948		25.2								
1949		31.6								
1950		35.0		25.5						
1951		41.6		27.7						
1952		46.3		31.3						
1953		43.8		36.9	31.4	0.5	6.6	25.3	21.0	2.0
1954		48.5		36.2	29.3	0.8	6.3	23.8	21.5	3.4
1955		58.2		40.6	32.6	0.7	6.7	26.6	20.6	2.6
1956	65.3	62.8	96.1	48.4	39.9	0.9	8.0	32.8	20.1	2.7
1957	70.4	66.1	93.9	51.5	43.4	1.0	9.5	34.9	21.9	2.9
1958	74.6	64.1	85.9	53.2	45.4	1.2	9.9	36.7	21.8	3.3
1959	77.9	69.8	89.6	51.8	44.0	1.2	10.4	34.8	23.6	3.4
1960	84.3	80.6	95.5	55.9	48.2	1.2	11.6	37.8	24.1	3.2
1961	88.4	81.0	91.7	65.5	56.0	2.1	11.8	46.3	21.1	4.5
1962	92.0	80.5	87.5	68.4	56.3	2.1	11.4	47.0	20.2	4.5
1963	96.8	80.7	83.3	70.2	56.6	2.7	10.3	49.0	18.2	5.5
1964	101.5	91.3	90.0	71.3	57.3	3.6	10.0	50.9	17.5	7.1
1965	112.5	94.7	84.2	78.2	64.5	2.9	11.6	55.8	18.0	5.2
1966	119.7	93.8	78.4	76.8	66.5	2.1	15.7	52.9	23.6	4.0

Source: Statistical Office of the European Communities, *Eisen und Stahl, Jahrbuch 1966*, pp. 6, 11, 46, and 266.

[a] From and to third countries.

[b] Apparent consumption = output + imports − exports. Rolling mill products converted to raw steel equivalents.

output in 1940 had totaled 36 million tons in the ECSC countries, with West Germany accounting for 24 million tons, or two-thirds of the total.

In 1946, raw steel output was a dismal 14 million tons; and though it increased sharply thereafter, the 1940 volume of production was not exceeded until 1951, when output reached 41.6 million tons.[3] The year 1951 is a banner year in the economic history of western Europe; the Coal and Steel Treaty among West Germany, France, Italy, Belgium, Luxembourg, and the Netherlands was signed, creating the European Coal and Steel Community—a forerunner of later, more extensive economic integration among the Six.

The record of the ECSC in its fifteen years of operation is complex and by no means capable of easy summary or evaluation. For the terms of reference of the present study, the following factors stand out:

(a) Since formation of the ECSC, steel output has surged ahead rapidly from 41.6 million tons, reaching 70 million tons in 1959 and thereafter stabilizing at 80 million tons annually from 1960 to 1963. From 1964 to 1966, output exceeded 90 million tons annually and averaged 93.3 million tons.

(b) Although steel demand within the Six also increased rapidly, with consumption rising from 31 million tons in 1951 to 77 million tons in 1965, available capacity increased even faster. As a result, the ECSC group found itself with a rising margin of excess capacity after 1961, which would have been even greater except for an important push of exports into third markets.

The output ratio was at 90 percent or higher from 1956 to 1961 (with the exception of 1958, when it fell to 86 percent); since then it has gradually declined. As Table 37 shows, it reached the 90 percent mark only once in the last five years, and in 1966 it fell to a new low of 78.4 percent. The details for the six individual members show (Table 38) that with the exception of Luxembourg—whose operating ratio has remained consistently above 90 percent—the excess capacity in raw steel production facilities has been generally diffused among the other five members of the ECSC. In terms of ten-year averages (1956 to 1965), the Luxembourg operating ratio was 95.1 percent. France was next with 91.9 percent, and the remaining Community members ranged between 87 and 89 percent, with actual ratios in 1965 and 1966 falling below the ten-year averages. As available trade statistics combine Belgium and Luxembourg data, it is not possible to determine to what extent intra-Community trade is helpful to the maintenance of high operating ratios for Luxembourg, though the relatively heavy flow of ingots and semi-

[3]Unless otherwise indicated, all data in this section are from the Statistical Bureau of the European Communities, *Eisen und Stahl, 1966, Jahrbuch.* All figures in metric tons have been converted to net tons of 2,000 pounds.

TABLE 38

RATIO OF RAW STEEL OUTPUT TO CAPACITY, ECSC MEMBERS, 1956–66

	West Germany	France	Italy	Netherlands	Belgium	Luxembourg	ECSC
1956	97.8	95.0	92.6	97.3	93.8	98.5	96.1
1957	95.2	94.6	91.5	93.3	87.9	97.0	93.9
1958	83.7	93.4	80.1	92.5	80.8	93.6	85.9
1959	89.4	93.9	84.3	90.4	84.6	93.7	89.6
1960	96.5	96.7	94.3	93.5	88.9	98.6	95.5
1961	90.7	94.7	93.0	90.2	84.8	97.7	91.7
1962	85.6	88.1	91.4	82.2	87.9	93.7	87.5
1963	79.5	84.0	92.5	79.7	85.1	90.3	83.3
1964	91.2	91.6	83.7	84.4	88.6	94.2	90.0
1965	80.9	86.5	84.6	88.8	87.5	93.5	84.2
1966							78.4

Source: *Eisen und Stahl, Jahrbuch, 1966*, pp. 10–11.

finished steel from the Belgium-Luxembourg Economic Union into the rest of the Community (almost one million net tons in 1965) points in this direction.

The capacity and demand projections for the ECSC in a recent OECD study show little change in the ratio of capacity utilization by 1970. Capacity in that year is estimated at 132 million tons, compared with expected production of 105 million tons, leaving an unused margin of 27 million tons, or 20 percent. The underlying details for domestic demand and net exports have not been published.

(c) Since the establishment of the ECSC, the sharp rise in intra-Community trade from 2 million tons in 1952 to 13 million tons in 1965 (almost 30 percent of total Atlantic trade; see Table 32) has been a major factor in the over-all rise in world steel trade. Among the Six, Belgium-Luxembourg presently remains the only net exporter in intra-Community trade, with other members purchasing tonnages ranging from 900,000 tons to 1.2 million tons in 1965.

Intra-Community trade partly reflects vertical imbalances among individual companies of various countries, as shown by flows of ingot and semi-finished steel. Trade in these products rose from 500,000 net tons in 1953 to 2.6 million tons in 1965. Such trade was a two-way proposition for West Germany, France, Belgium-Luxembourg, and, to a lesser degree, the Netherlands, while Italy was a relatively large importer (as Table 39 shows).

However, although the increase in trade in ingot and semi-finished steel has been rapid in the period under review, it was only moderately faster than the rise in rolling-mill-product trade, which amounted to 2.4 million net tons

TABLE 39

INTRA-FCSC TRADE IN INGOT AND SEMI-FINISHED STEEL, 1965
(thousands of net tons)

	Exported from					
Imported into	West Germany	France	Belgium-Luxembourg	Italy	Netherlands	Total ECSC
West Germany	—	129	328	6	21	484
France	513	—	482	—	23	1,018
Belgium-Luxembourg	68	141	—	—	160	369
Italy	270	213	107	—	53	643
Netherlands	37	2	55	—	—	94
ECSC total	888	485	972	6	257	2,608

Source: United Nations, ECE, *Statistics of World Trade in Steel, 1965.*

in 1953 and 10.4 million net tons in 1965.

(d) Historically, the ECSC countries have been net exporters of steel. Before World War II most of the member countries (West Germany, France, Belgium, and Luxembourg) had built up a sizable volume of steel export trade. After the initial reconstruction, rolling-mill-product exports to third countries by the ECSC averaged 6.5 million tons between 1952 and 1954. They reached 10 million tons in 1957 and remained in a 10- to 11.5-million-ton range from then until 1964. In 1965 exports to third countries spurted ahead to 15.7 million tons.

As our export and import tables (Tables 30–32) show, the geographical structure of ECSC exports is widely diversified. In 1965, 2 percent of all shipments to third countries went to the United Kingdom, 23 percent to the other EFTA countries, 23 percent to the United States, 5 percent to Canada, and the remaining 46 percent were widely scattered over Africa, Asia, and the Middle East.

(e) Imports from outside the Community have increased from 500,000 tons in 1952 (rolling mill products) to a peak of 3.6 million tons in 1963, following which they declined to 2.1 million tons in 1965. The geographical distribution of ECSC imports from third countries is shown in Tables 30–32. They originate mainly from the major EFTA producers (the United Kingdom, Austria, Sweden, and Norway), and the second largest source of supply is some of the Communist countries of eastern Europe. By comparison, other sources of supply are not significant. Imports from the United States ranged between 300,000 and 400,000 tons in the mid-1950s and have since declined to less than 100,000 tons. Imports from Canada never exceeded the 100,000-ton mark and, after a brief flurry between 1960 and

1963, have been at token quantities. Shipments appeared from Japan in 1962, but after a 1963 peak level of 500,000 tons, they declined to less than 200,000 tons by 1965.

A surge of imports from the Communist countries in eastern Europe took place in the 1960s, with the volume rising from 200,000 tons per year in the late 1950s to a peak of one million tons in 1963. Since then these imports have declined to 500,000 tons in 1965, but their impact on the ECSC's commercial policy was significant. The prices at which the eastern European steel entered the ECSC were substantially below those prevailing in the Community's domestic markets and consequently had an unsettling effect on steel-market conditions. The combination of a reduced rate of growth in the demand for steel after 1962 and the emergence of excess capacity in the ECSC resulted in the February, 1964, recommendation by the ECSC High Authority that the member states should raise their tariffs on most steel products to the Italian tariff (the highest among the Six) and prohibit price alignment on imports from state trading countries.[4]

The geographical origin of imports from third countries into the ECSC thus is heavily European, with North American and Japanese sources contributing only a small portion, amounting to approximately 10 percent, of imports from all third countries in 1965.

(f) Since the mid-1950s, the ECSC group has become a large net steel exporter. Net exports increased from approximately 6 million tons in the early 1950s to some 9 million tons at the end of the decade and finally spurted ahead to 13.6 million tons in 1965.

Compared to Canada and the United States, exports by the ECSC account for a significant share of total shipments. Measured by rolling-mill-product delivery statistics compiled by the Community since 1952, exports as a percentage of total shipments have fluctuated around a ratio of 20 percent, ranging from highs of about 24 percent in 1958, 1959, and 1965 to lows of 18 percent from 1962 to 1964. In 1965 they amounted to 23.6 percent of total shipments. The relatively high ratio of exports to total shipments has been maintained in the face of sharp increases in intra-ECSC trade and a substantial increase in domestic consumption of rolling mill products. The rising volume of exports also has helped to maintain the Community's steel-capacity utilization.

By comparison with this relatively high ratio of exports to total shipments, the ratio of imports from third countries to apparent consumption is small. During the 1950s it was a fairly steady 3 percent of consumption. In the 1960s it ranged between 4 and 6 percent in every year with the exception

---

[4]The tariff increases were alleviated by tariff quotas granted to the maximum extent found possible. OECD, *The Iron and Steel Industry in 1964*, p. 49.

of 1963, when, as the result of particularly heavy shipments from the eastern European countries, it rose to 7.1 percent.

The international trade position of the Community is thus fundamentally different from that of the North American countries. Compared to import penetration into the U.S. and Canadian markets, imports into Community countries have remained relatively small and are concentrated among individual ECSC members. (See Table 40.)

TABLE 40

ROLLING-MILL-PRODUCT IMPORTS BY ECSC MEMBERS, 1965
(millions of net tons)

	Imports		
	From other ECSC members	From third countries	Total
West Germany	4.4	1.2	5.6
France	3.9	0.2	4.1
Belgium-Luxembourg	1.1	0.2	1.3
Italy	1.5	0.5	2.0
Netherlands	2.0	0.3	2.3
Total	12.9	2.4	15.3

Source: U.N., ECE, *Statistics of World Trade in Steel, 1965.*

Among the Community members, imports from third countries are mostly confined to West Germany and to Italy (in the case of Italy, this is expected to decrease after 1965 as the result of a large expansion in domestic production facilities). By origin, this trade is also highly concentrated in Austrian shipments to West Germany and, during the upsurge of shipments from eastern European countries, in imports to West Germany, Italy, and the Netherlands.

The export structure of the ECSC is highly diversified by geographical destination and reaches all the rest of the industrial world with the exception of Japan.

Among the individual Community members, exports in 1965 were distributed as shown in Table 41. West Germany and Belgium-Luxembourg are by far the largest exporters to third countries. For intra-Community trade, Belgium-Luxembourg is the only net exporter, with the four other countries showing net import balances.

In terms of exports to third countries in 1965, West Germany and Belgium-Luxembourg led the way with shipments exceeding 5 million tons

TABLE 41

EXPORTS OF ROLLING MILL PRODUCTS BY MEMBERS OF THE ECSC, 1965
(millions of net tons)

	Exports		
	To other members	To third countries	Total
West Germany	3.9	5.2	9.1
France	2.9	3.6	6.5
Belgium-Luxembourg	4.8	5.1	9.9
Italy	0.6	1.5	2.1
Netherlands	0.8	1.1	1.9
Total	13.0	16.5	29.5

Source: See Table 40.

in 1965. France is next with 3.6 million tons, followed by Italy (1.5 million tons) and the Netherlands (1.1 million tons).

On a net basis (after taking imports shown in Table 40 into account), Belgium-Luxembourg emerges as the dominant net exporter with 8.6 million tons. It is followed by West Germany (3.5 million tons) and France (2.4 million tons). Italy's trade is virtually balanced (net exports of 100,000 tons), while the Netherlands show net imports of 400,000 tons.

Both the large expansion in intra-Community trade and the rising net exports of the ECSC to third countries are major factors in the world steel-trading picture today. In 1965, intra-Community trade accounted for 22.7 percent of world trade. The Community's exports were 28.9 percent of the world total, excluding intra-Community trade.

These figures influence the commercial-policy stance of the Community countries, and as such they become a major factor in our subsequent evaluations. (See pages 130 and 134.)

C. JAPAN[5]

The growth of the Japanese steel industry in the postwar period dwarfs the performance of any other nation's steel industry. From a prewar level of output of some 7 million tons of raw steel and early postwar lows of one million tons or less in 1946 and 1947, the industry expanded its production of raw steel to 10 million tons by 1955, nearly 25 million tons in 1960, and

[5]Unless otherwise indicated, the data in this section are based on Table 42, compiled from the Japan Iron and Steel Federation's *Statistical Year Book for 1965 and 1967*.

52.7 million tons in 1966. Output of rolled steel products exceeded 5 million tons in 1951. It increased to almost 11 million tons in 1957, 24 million tons in 1962, almost 42 million tons in 1966, and 54 million tons in 1967 (Table 42). The ratio of Japanese to non-Communist world steel production increased from 1.5 percent in 1947–49 to 14.4 percent in 1966 (Table 29). The surge combines the following elements:

(a) A sharp rate of growth in domestic steel use, with apparent consumption increasing from an average of approximately 4 million tons of rolled steel products in the period 1950 to 1952 to more than 10 million tons in 1957, 21.5 million tons in 1961, 31.9 million tons in 1966, and 45.1 million tons in 1967. The rise in steel use combines the requirements for domestic consumption and supplies to steel-using export industries (for example, shipbuilding, machinery, and automobiles).

(b) Japanese steel exports before World War II were in a range of 700,000 to 800,000 tons of rolling mill products (from 12 to 15 percent of total output); and following the initial postwar reconstruction period, exports rapidly began to be a significant part of the industry's total output. Rolling-mill-product exports (excluding products of a more advanced manufacture, such as steel pipe) were generally in a range of 1 to 1.5 million tons during 1951 to 1959 and fluctuated between 8 and 25 percent of total production, averaging 12.5 percent in this period. In absolute terms, exports increased sharply during the 1960s, rising from 2.2 million tons in 1960 and 1961 to 9.5 million tons in 1965.[6] The percentage of total production accounted for by exports increased from 12 percent in 1960 to 20 percent in 1964 and 26.5 percent in 1965. In terms of the world trading data shown in Tables 30 and 32, the ratio of Japanese net steel exports to total world exports increased from 2.4 percent in 1953 to 15.2 percent in 1965.

The 1964 and 1965 increases pushed exports to sharply higher peaks; and particularly in the face of a decline in domestic demand during 1965, export sales became a significant factor in maintaining total output and a high ratio in relation to available capacity.[7] At an annual level exceeding nine million tons in 1965, Japanese steel exports rank second only to the combined net export position of the ECSC in world steel markets.

(c) By comparison with the important position exports occupy in the Japanese steel industry's operations, imports are a small factor in the

[6]This export total is based upon statistics compiled by the Japan Iron and Steel Federation (see Table 42). It is somewhat more inclusive than the rolling-mill-product figures appearing in Tables 30 and 32, which are based on ECE compilations.
[7]In 1966 exports were 9.7 million tons and 23.3 percent of rolled steel output. In 1967 the respective figures were 9.1 million tons and 16.8 percent.

TABLE 42

STEEL INDUSTRY AND MARKET DATA, JAPAN, 1947–67

(volume figures in millions of net tons)

	Raw steel			Rolled steel products					
	Capacity	Output	Operating ratio	Output	Exports	Imports	Apparent consumption	Exports as a percentage of output	Imports as a percentage of apparent consumption
1947		1.0		0.7	a	a	0.7		
1948		1.9		1.3	a	a	1.3	1.2	0.2
1949		3.4		2.4	0.2	a	2.2	8.3	0.3
1950		5.3		3.9	0.4	a	3.5	11.2	0.0
1951		7.2		5.4	0.9	a	4.5	16.7	0.6
1952		7.7		5.6	1.4	a	4.2	25.6	0.6
1953		8.4		6.2	0.7	0.1	5.6	11.4	1.8
1954		8.5		6.4	1.0	0.1	5.5	15.8	1.6
1955		10.4		7.9	1.4	0.1	6.6	18.3	1.0
1956	12.4	12.2	98.3	9.5	1.0	0.2	8.7	10.6	2.4
1957	16.9	13.9	82.3	10.9	0.9	1.1	11.1	8.2	9.7
1958	18.3	13.4	73.2	10.4	1.6	0.2	9.0	15.1	1.7
1959	20.9	18.3	87.6	14.0	1.6	0.3	12.7	11.1	2.7
1960	24.4	24.4	100.0	18.6	2.2	0.4	16.8	12.0	2.2
1961	30.1	31.2	103.7	23.6	2.2	0.2	21.6	9.5	1.1
1962	33.9	30.4	89.7	24.0	3.8	0.1	20.3	15.8	0.3
1963	39.7	34.7	87.4	27.5	5.1	a	22.4	18.5	0.2
1964	46.0	43.9	95.4	34.3	6.6	a	27.7	19.7	0.1
1965	48.8	45.4	93.0	35.8	9.5	a	26.3	26.5	0.1
1966	52.3	52.7	100.8	41.6	9.7	a	31.9	23.3	0.1
1967		68.5		54.1	9.1	0.1	45.1	16.8	0.2

Sources: The Japan Iron and Steel Federation, *Statistical Year Book for 1965 and 1967.*

a Less than 50,000 tons.

Japanese steel market, amounting typically to less than 2 percent of apparent consumption and to less than that during recent years. The year 1957 is an exception, as more than one million tons of rolling mill products were imported from the United States, some ECSC members (West Germany, Belgium-Luxembourg), and Australia, mostly in sheets, plate, and heavy structurals. This unusually high volume of imports, and purchases ranging from 200,000 to 300,000 tons annually between 1956 and 1961 (ranging from one to 3 percent of apparent consumption in the other years), reflected shortages in Japanese production facilities as domestic consumption rose rapidly in this period (see Table 42).

Imports during recent years have been nominal—amounting to less than 100,000 tons and in a range of 0.1 to 0.3 percent of apparent consumption between 1962 and 1966. Interestingly, a vertical imbalance in the Japanese steel industry appeared during the 1960s, leading to sizable imports of pig iron, ranging from 1.1 million tons in 1960 to a peak of 3.7 million tons in 1964. Recent expansion of blast furnace capacity is expected to eliminate most of these imports.

Japanese iron and steel imports appear to reflect entirely past deficits in capacity or vertical imbalances. By comparison with import patterns in other major producing countries, the Japanese steel industry has not been faced with price-competitive imports, even with the rise in international competitive pressures. This fact differentiates the Japanese steel market from that of North America; it comes closer to the ECSC position, though the Europeans experienced the impact of eastern European exports. Furthermore, some ECSC countries (particularly West Germany) conduct a substantial volume of bilateral trade with some EFTA members (Austria and the United Kingdom). No corresponding flows are found in the Japanese situation.

(d) The Japanese position in world steel markets has thus become one of a dominant exporter. In view of its dependence on imported raw materials for steel production and of the emphasis on building up steel-consuming export industries, it is by no means clear to what extent a long-run buildup in exports of rolling mill products will take place. Speaking at the recent International Iron and Steel Institute meeting in Brussels, the president of Yawata Iron and Steel Company stated that Japan intends to shift its emphasis away from primary iron and steel to more finished products made of steel.[8] Although this might stabilize or cut the level of Japanese rolling-mill-product exports, the impact would feed back on the importing nations' steel industries through the volume of the derived demand for domestic steel products.

[8]*American Metal Market*, Nov. 13, 1967, p. 5.

D. UNITED KINGDOM[9]

By comparison with most of the other large steel-producing nations, the output of steel in the United Kingdom has advanced moderately in the postwar period. Production of raw steel amounted to 13.2 million net tons in 1945; it rose to 18.2 million tons in 1950 and nearly 20 million tons in 1953. The peak for the 1950s was 24.3 million tons in 1957. During the 1960s, output reached successively higher levels; the new peak of 27.2 million tons in 1960 held until 1964, when production amounted to 29.4 million tons; in 1965 production reached 30.2 million tons. Following this, there were declines to 27.2 million tons in 1966 and 26.8 million tons in 1967. The ratio of production to capacity was generally high until the mid-1950s; it amounted to 97 percent in 1953 and 98 percent in 1955. As can be seen in Table 43, the degree of capacity utilization declined subsequently, falling to a low of 74 percent in 1962. In 1964 and 1965 it rose to 87 percent, but fell again to 79 percent in 1966.

The long-term position of the United Kingdom's steel industry is not easy to assess. Domestically, a sluggish growth in the economy has had a dampening impact on steel demand, with an annual rise in steel consumption of only 1.9 percent in the years 1954 to 1963. Even though home demand improved in 1964 and 1965 (rising to 27 million net tons of ingot equivalent compared to 22 million tons in 1963), the apparent consumption gains of the United Kingdom are the smallest for any of the major countries, except the United States.

Foreign trade volumes have been hardly more dynamic, either on the export or the import side. Over-all, the United Kingdom has maintained a consistent net steel export position, resulting from exports ranging from 3.3 to 4.7 million net tons (ingot equivalent) from 1954 to 1965, compared with imports in the range of 0.6 and 2.0 million tons. Additional data are shown in Table 43. From 1954 to 1963, imports as a percentage of apparent consumption ranged from a low of 3 percent (in 1954, 1958, 1959, and 1961) to a high of 10 percent (in 1955). By comparison, exports have moved upward in a relatively narrow range, starting at 16 percent of total production in 1954 and gradually increasing to 19 percent by 1962 and 1963.

The deterioration in the international competitive position of British manufactured goods during the postwar period is not significantly reflected in the steel-trade data. In spite of the rise in the steel exports of the ECSC and Japan, the British share of rolling-mill-product exports of the fifteen of the largest steel-producing countries[10] declined only moderately in the decade

[9]The statistics up to 1963 pertaining to the United Kingdom are from the Iron and Steel Board, *Development in the Iron and Steel Industry, Special Report, 1964*, p. 21.
[10]The ECSC group, Japan, the United States, Sweden, Australia, Austria, Norway, Canada, and South Africa.

TABLE 43

STEEL INDUSTRY AND MARKET DATA, UNITED KINGDOM, 1946–66
(volume figures in millions of net tons)

	Raw steel			Imports	Exports (ingot equivalent)	Consumption*	Imports as a percentage of consumption	Exports as a percentage of production
	Capacity	Output	Operating ratio					
1946		14.2						
1947		12.2						
1948		16.7						
1949		17.3						
1950	19.3	18.2	94.3					
1951		17.5						
1952		18.4						
1953	20.3	19.7	97.0					
1954		20.7		0.5	3.2	18.8	2.8	15.7
1955	22.6	22.2	98.2	2.1	3.8	20.0	10.4	17.0
1956		23.1		2.0	3.7	20.7	9.6	15.9
1957	25.1	24.3	96.8	1.1	4.1	21.2	5.0	16.8
1958	26.2	21.9	83.6	0.6	3.5	20.2	3.2	16.1
1959	26.6	22.6	85.0	0.6	3.9	20.3	2.8	17.2
1960	28.9	27.2	94.1	1.8	4.4	22.8	7.9	16.0
1961	29.7	24.7	83.2	0.6	4.5	21.9	2.9	18.1
1962	31.1	23.0	74.0	1.1	4.4	21.0	5.2	19.3
1963	32.3	25.2	78.0	1.7	4.8	22.8	7.7	19.1
1964	33.6	29.4	87.5	2.7	4.9	27.2	9.9	16.7
1965	34.7	30.2	87.0	1.0	4.7	26.5	3.8	15.6
1966	34.5	27.2	78.8					

Sources: 1954–63: Iron and Steel Board, *Development in the Iron and Steel Industry, Special Report, 1964*. Other years: U.S. Senate, *Steel Import Study*; OECD, and ECE.
Note: (1) 1964–65 imports and exports, and ratio calculations based on ECE trade data using conversion factors of 0.7.
(2) Percentage calculations made from unrounded data.
*Including inventory changes 1954–63.

from 1954 to 1963 (see Table 44). The steel-trade data available for 1964 and 1965 from the OECD and ECE (see Table 32) show that the above patterns continued. Exports of rolled steel products averaged 3.5 million net tons in 1964 and 1965, compared with 3.1 million tons in 1963. Imports, following a 1964 increase, dropped sharply in 1965, leaving the United Kingdom with an export balance of 3 million net tons.

TABLE 44

RATIO OF U.K. EXPORTS OF STEEL TO
THE TOTAL OF FIFTEEN OF THE
LARGEST STEEL-PRODUCING
COUNTRIES, 1954–63

Three-year averages	Percentage
1954–56	14.0
1957–59	13.1
1960–62	12.7
1963	12.8

Source: Iron and Steel Board, *Development in the Iron and Steel Industry, Special Report 1964,* Table 14, p. 29.

British imports originate mainly in the ECSC and other EFTA members, with smaller tonnages coming in from the United States, Canada, Australia, and some of the eastern European countries. The structure of British export trade is more diffused, though the ECSC and the EFTA countries are important purchasers. Other important customers in recent years include the United States, Canada, India, South Africa, and Argentina.

The outlook for British steel exports over the long run is not clear-cut. The decline in the British share of the total world market that occurred between 1954 and 1964 appears attributable to the fact that "countries whose imports of steel are declining or are stationary had traditionally been quantitatively more important markets for Britain than for her competitors."[11] Looking to 1970, the same study concluded that "British exports of steel seem likely to fluctuate from year to year, but on balance it seems unlikely that they will grow much further in the period up to 1970. Exports in 1970 may amount to about 3.6 million tons product weight or 5.0 million tons ingot equivalent."[12]

Imports from 1945 to the end of the 1950s largely represented deficiencies

[11]Iron and Steel Board, *Development in the Iron and Steel Industry,* p. 32.
[12]*Ibid.*

in domestic supply. The share of domestic consumption supplied by imports fluctuated in the 1950s in a range of about 3 to 10 percent, depending upon the level of domestic demand. The low level of imports in 1958 and 1959 reflected a domestic recession in steel demand. After 1960 the situation changed as the industry's capacity expanded sufficiently to meet foreseeable demand. Combined with a recession in domestic steel demand from the middle of 1961 to mid-1963, the need for deficit-covering imports was reduced. In 1961, total imports fell to 600,000 net tons (ingot equivalent), including almost 70,000 tons of materials for hire-rolling.

The rise in excess capacity in other major steel-producing countries was evidenced in the British market by offers of surplus production at prices that were highly competitive with those of domestic producers and often below those in the country of origin, and this was the main reason for the increase in British imports after 1961.[13] The 1965 trade figures showed a reversal of pattern, as imports fell to the lowest level since 1961, but a new rise in imports during 1966 brought the total back to the one-million-ton level again.[14]

By geographical origin, the major change in import sources was a decline in shipments from the United States after the mid-1950s. These were replaced by rising shipments from EFTA and Commonwealth countries. By comparison, shipments from the European Coal and Steel Community have fluctuated trendlessly, though the Community remains the largest supplier to the British market. The Iron and Steel Board concluded that by 1970 British imports would amount to one million net tons of rolling mill products. This would mean about the same level of imports as in 1963, but less than in 1964. The projection assumed that there would be no significant changes in relative levels of national steel tariffs, but a planned further reduction of tariffs within the EFTA countries.[15]

More recently, two other major changes enter into the picture of the British steel industry in the international context. In July, 1967, the industry was renationalized, as the British Steel Corporation took over fourteen of the largest crude-steel producers with a capacity of close to 32 million net tons, representing 93.5 percent of the country's steel-making capacity. Although the nationalized company controls most of Britain's steel facilities, 210 companies were left in the private sector. These produce a very small percentage of the carbon steels, but a relatively high percentage of specialty products.[16]

For operations and sales purposes, the nationalized industry has been

13*Ibid.*, p. 33.
14*American Metal Market*, Aug. 11, 1967.
15Iron and Steel Board, *Development in the Iron and Steel Industry*, p. 34.
16*American Metal Market*, July 27, 1967, pp. 1 and 11. The nationalization cut-off point was 475,000 tons of crude capacity.

organized into four regional divisions, among which there will be no price competition. The groups will charge identical prices, which will be set and published after consultation among the four regional groups and the central organization.[17]

Renationalization raises a number of important questions for this study. First, how will a state-run industry behave in the market place? Judging from the "loyalty rebates" that went into effect in January, 1968 (see page 125), it may well be inward-looking. Will greater rationalization and better efficiency of the nationalized industry be achieved, and how would this alter the international competitive position of British steel? To raise this point is in itself optimistic. Beyond this, the November, 1967, devaluation of the British pound now enters the picture. Even after allowances for higher costs of imported raw materials, British steel has been given a competitive boost upward of 10 percent, both in attempting to establish a broader base of exports and in meeting import competition. To date, British Steel Corporation's export policy appears to have been to leave its export prices unchanged, in an attempt to make overseas sales more profitable.[18]

E. OTHER EFTA COUNTRIES

The other EFTA countries—Austria, Denmark, Norway, Portugal, Sweden, and Switzerland—round out the list of countries included in our Atlantic nations survey. In total size, the group is a relatively small factor in the world steel picture, with output first exceeding the ten-million-ton mark in 1964 (approximately similar in size to that of Canada).

Prewar, among the six countries in the group, only Austria and Sweden had established steel industries, with output levels of approximately one million tons. Norway's production was 100,000 tons, while no steel industry existed in the other three countries. Production of the other EFTA group steadily improved in the postwar period. Output of raw steel averaged 2.3 million tons from 1947 to 1949, with Austria and Sweden accounting for 90 percent of the total. Small productive capacities were installed after the war in Denmark (1947), Switzerland (1954), and Portugal (1961); but even by the mid-1960s the capacity of these three countries totaled only 1.2 million tons. Meanwhile, Austria and Sweden expanded their industries rapidly, while that of Norway was also gradually built up. As a result, output rose to the 5-million-ton level for the first time in 1955, when the combined capacity of the group was 5.5 million tons.

From there on, a substantial expansion in the group's steel industries continued until 1965. Austrian output, which reached the 1-million-ton mark

[17]*American Metal Market*, Aug. 11, 1967, pp. 1 and 20.
[18]*Ibid.*, Jan. 5, 1968, pp. 1 and 19.

TABLE 45

STEEL INDUSTRY AND MARKET DATA, OTHER EFTA COUNTRIES,* 1946–66
(volume figures in millions of net tons)

	Raw steel			Rolling mill products					
	Capacity	Output	Operating ratio	Output	Imports (net)†	Exports (net)†	Apparent consumption	Net imports as a percentage of apparent consumption	Net exports as a percentage of production
1946		1.6							
1947		1.9							
1948		2.3							
1949		2.7							
1950		2.9							
1951		3.1							
1952		3.4							
1953		3.7							
1954		4.3			1.7	0.5			
1955	5.5	5.0	90.9		2.3	0.6			
1956		5.8			2.9	0.7			
1957		6.3			2.6	1.0			
1958	6.9	6.2	89.9		2.7	1.4			
1959		7.0		4.2	2.2	1.2	5.2	42.3	28.6
1960	8.2	8.1	98.8	4.8	2.5	1.0	6.3	39.7	20.8
1961	9.1	8.7	95.6	5.6	3.5	1.6	7.5	46.7	28.6
1962	9.5	8.9	93.7	6.0	3.7	1.8	7.9	46.8	30.0
1963	9.9	9.3	93.9	6.3	3.6	1.7	8.2	43.9	27.0
1964	10.2	10.2	100.0	6.6	3.5	1.8	8.3	42.2	27.3
1965	11.1	10.8	97.3	7.5	4.4	2.4	9.5	46.3	32.0
1966	11.6	10.8	93.1	7.8	4.7	1.9	10.6	44.3	24.4

Sources: U.S. Senate, *Steel Import Study*; ECE, *The European Steel Market*; and OECD, *The Iron and Steel Industry* (annual issues).
*Austria, Denmark, Norway, Portugal, Sweden, and Switzerland.
†To third countries.

in 1950 and 2 million tons in 1955, rose to a level of 3.5 million tons in the mid-1960s. Swedish production, which had averaged 1.5 million tons from 1949 to 1951, rose to 3.1 million tons in 1959 and passed the 5-million-ton mark in 1965 and 1966. The new industries of the other three countries achieved a relatively stable level of output in the 1960s of slightly more than one million tons.

As a group, the other EFTA countries' production rose from an early postwar average of 2.3 million tons in 1947–59 to 5 million tons in 1955, 8.1 million tons in 1960, and 10.8 million tons in 1966. Although a relatively small factor in the Atlantic steel picture, output of the group rose from 1.7 percent after the war to 3.0 percent currently.

The ratio of capacity utilization was 90 percent in 1955 and 1958 and has remained above that ratio throughout the 1960s (for details see Table 45). This relatively high degree of utilization by the other EFTA group is in distinct contrast with the situation in the ECSC and the United Kingdom.

The volumes of trade by the other EFTA group are large in relation to output and apparent steel consumption. Exports as a percentage of output of rolling mill products were 21 percent in 1959 and 24 percent in 1965. Similarly, imports as a ratio to apparent consumption were 40 percent and 44 percent, respectively.

The rise in the volume of exports and imports can be seen from the comparative data for 1953, 1959, and 1965 given in Table 46.

Over-all, the other EFTA group remains a net importer of steel rolling mill products; this holds for all the individual countries, with the exception of Austria, which is a relatively large net exporter.

TABLE 46

STEEL TRADE OF "OTHER" EFTA COUNTRIES IN A WORLD PERSPECTIVE, 1953, 1959, AND 1965

(millions of net tons)

	Exports			Imports		
	1953	1959	1965	1953	1959	1965
Other EFTA	0.1	0.3	0.6	0.1	0.3	0.6
ECSC	0.2	0.6	1.0	1.3	2.4	3.8
United Kingdom	0.1	a	0.2	0.3	0.3	0.5
Other Atlantic	0.1	0.1	0.1	0.1	a	0.1
Rest of world	0.1	0.6	0.6	a	0.1	0.3
Total	0.6	1.6	2.5	1.8	3.1	5.3

Source: Tables 30 to 32.
aLess than 50,000 tons.

In geographical terms, the trade of the other EFTA group is oriented towards Europe. The largest exports and imports are with the ECSC, and here the volume of West German–Austrian trade is a significant part of the total. Interestingly, intra-EFTA trade (including the United Kingdom) is not in a dominant position among the totals: it amounted to less than one-third of all exports in 1965 and slightly more than 20 percent of total imports. The trading relationships seem to be more significantly influenced by the presence of the large ECSC steel industries, particularly in contiguous territories. Trade with Canada has been in token quantities; the same generally applies to Japan and the United States.

F. CANADIAN STEEL-TRADE TRENDS

Table 47 summarizes the over-all results of Canadian international trade in steel during the postwar period, in terms of the ratios of imports to apparent consumption and of exports to total Canadian mill shipments. The five-year averages are based on tonnages shown separately in Table 48.[19] The ratio of imports to apparent consumption shows a downward trend throughout the postwar period, with successive five-year averages declining from 27.2 percent in 1947 to 1951, to 25.7 percent from 1952 to 1956, 20.7 percent from 1957 to 1961, and finally 17.2 percent from 1962 to 1966. Along the way, imports in 1962 and 1963, with respective ratios of 12.0 and 13.3 percent, were the lowest on record and indicative of the extent to which the Canadian industry could supply domestic requirements under conditions of normal cyclical expansion. By contrast, the higher ratios of the period 1964 and 1965 in part reflected peak cyclical demands under the conditions of extremely rapid rates of growth in business investment expenditures. In 1966 and 1967, imports amounted to 16.2 percent of apparent consumption.

The figures for total rolling-mill-product imports average out large differences among individual product groups. The sharpest displacement of imports has been among the product groups for which the market shows the most rapid growth: flat-hot-rolled and flat-cold-rolled products. In addition, the high ratio of imports to apparent consumption in the heavy-structural product group has also been reduced. In two other product groups—bars and wire rods—the ratio of imports to apparent consumption has actually risen since 1953, and it is among these that the impact of price-competitive imports first became apparent. Imports in the remaining product categories (semi-finished steel shapes, rails, and track materials) are not significant in relation to total market requirements.

[19]The tonnages used here are derived from *Trade of Canada*, rather than the Economic Commission for Europe compilations used elsewhere. Table 49 is an exception in order to avoid lengthy computations involved for determining geographical details from the *Trade of Canada* data.

TABLE 47

IMPORTS AND EXPORTS OF STEEL ROLLING MILL PRODUCTS, CANADA, 1947–67
(Volume figures in thousands of net tons)

	Imports	Exports	Apparent consumption	Imports as a percentage of apparent consumption	Exports as a percentage of total Canadian mill shipments
1947	818	168	3,173	25.8	7.1
1948	779	243	3,402	22.9	9.3
1949	964	220	3,672	26.3	8.1
1950	834	219	3,667	22.7	7.7
1951	1,318	70	3,439	38.3	2.2
1952	1,187	82	4,326	27.4	2.6
1953	1,001	150	4,237	23.6	4.6
1954	764	61	3,330	22.9	2.4
1955	911	402	3,968	23.0	11.6
1956	1,612	194	5,471	29.5	4.8
1957	1,513	212	5,141	29.4	5.5
1958	979	223	4,117	23.8	6.6
1959	921	204	5,175	17.8	4.6
1960	843	666	4,515	18.7	14.8
1961	669	454	4,819	13.9	9.9
1962	618	609	5,132	12.0	11.9
1963	785	799	5,903	13.3	13.5
1964	1,349	784	7,275	18.5	11.7
1965	1,904	610	8,396	22.7	8.6
1966	1,248	673	7,704	16.2	9.4
1967	1,172	872	7,247	16.2	12.5
Averages					
1947–51	943	184	3,471	27.2	6.7
1952–56	1,095	178	4,266	25.7	5.4
1957–61	985	352	4,753	20.7	8.5
1962–66	1,181	695	6,882	17.2	10.9

Sources: 1947–54 and 1967: compiled from DBS, *Primary Iron and Steel*, cat. no. 41-001, annual December issues, and *Trade of Canada, Imports by Commodities*. 1955–66: Tables 10.1, 19, and 21 of the Algoma Supplement.
Note: Total Canadian mill shipments for the years 1955–67 are shown in Table 3.

Conditions of the steel market in Canada during 1964, 1965, and the early part of 1966 made it difficult to distinguish between shortages of supply and the pressure of price-competitive imports. The ratios of raw-steel-capacity utilization since 1961 suggest that, in the early parts of the long cyclical expansion, some slack existed in the domestic industry, as the ratio of capacity utilization averaged 90 percent for the years 1961 and 1962, although the volumes in proportion to total demand covered by imports were relatively small during those years. In the next three years, virtually full theoretical capacity utilization was achieved, with operating ratios of 100 percent in both 1963 and 1964, and 95 percent in 1965. The relatively high import-to-consumption ratios of 1964 (18.5 percent) and 1965 (22.7 percent) are evidence of a cyclical shortage of production facilities. This certainly applied to the rise in most flat-rolled-product imports (particularly skelp), though in those years the impact of price-competitive bar and rod imports was already being felt.

The results for 1966 and 1967 point to different conclusions. The output figures for both years are influenced by production losses as a result of strikes against one of the major producers. But the operating rates of 87 percent in 1966 and 82 percent in 1967, combined with rolling-mill-product imports totaling 1.2 million tons and 16 percent of apparent consumption in each year, raise the question of the growing presence of price-competitive imports in the Canadian steel market after the peak demands of the cycle subsided. This is partly reflected also by the entry of steel from a number of overseas countries such as Australia, Czechoslovakia, and Poland which heretofore had not been suppliers of any consequence in the Canadian market.

Although evidence of some price-competitive imports into the Canadian steel market has existed for a number of years, the over-all impact has been small and partly concealed by the shortfall of available capacity in relation to the size of the market and its growth. For example, the volume of rod imports has risen consistently in the last decade (this was one of the first product groups in which the pressure of excess capacity was felt), and the ratio of the share of imports to apparent consumption increased from less than 5 percent in the mid-1950s to more than 25 percent of the market in the last two years. There is a similar, though less pronounced, upward trend in the ratio of imports of bar-size structural shapes and concrete-reinforcing bars.

The question raised by these and other patterns arising in the 1966 and 1967 imports is whether the Canadian steel market, though small in absolute size, is now beginning to feel more generally the competitive pressure of the rising excess steel capacity in the world, a form of competition the U.S. market has experienced for a number of years.

The ratio of imports to consumption on a national basis also shows relatively wide geographical dispersion. As one might expect, the highest penetration of imports exists in British Columbia, where the delivered prices from the integrated mills in eastern Canada include high transport costs. As Table 48 shows, the ratio of imports to total apparent consumption of rolling mill products in British Columbia averaged 38.2 percent in the years 1961 to 1965, more than twice the national average of 16.9 percent. The second highest ratio is found in Quebec, with a ratio of 26.6 percent in the same period, reflecting the accessibility of Montreal to imports from overseas. The Atlantic region, though a relatively small user of steel, is next with an average of 18.2 percent of total consumption, again because of the accessi-

TABLE 48

RATIO OF STEEL ROLLING MILL IMPORTS TO APPARENT CONSUMPTION,
CANADA, BY REGION, 1961–65

	1961	1962	1963	1964	1965	1961–65 average
Atlantic provinces	17.7	11.3	15.8	19.6	23.0	18.2
Quebec	23.8	20.1	22.5	27.4	34.4	26.6
Ontario	9.8	8.6	10.0	14.6	17.4	12.8
Prairie provinces	8.0	5.2	3.3	16.1	8.3	8.7
British Columbia	31.3	30.1	31.8	33.7	52.4	38.2
Canada	13.9	12.0	13.3	18.5	22.7	16.9

Source: Computed from Table 13.1 of the Algoma Supplement.

bility of its ports to ocean-going vessels. By comparison, Ontario has a 12.8 percent import ratio, and the Prairie provinces an 8.7 percent ratio, for the same period.

Table 49 shows the geographical origin of Canadian steel imports annually for the years 1953 to 1966. In 1956, the peak year for imports during the 1950s, with total imports of 1.6 million tons, the United States accounted for 72.4 percent of all Canadian imports. The rest of the imports for that year were scattered among the ECSC countries (15.3 percent), the United Kingdom (10.3 percent), Japan (1.4 percent), and other countries (0.6 percent). By comparison, in 1965, the peak import year during the 1960s, when imports totaled 1.9 million tons, the United States accounted for 28.2 percent, the ECSC for 48.6 percent, the United Kingdom for 10.2 percent, Japan for 10.4 percent, and the rest of the world for 2.6 percent.

This relative decline in the share of U.S. exports continued in 1966, when they fell to 28 percent of a 1.2-million-ton total. The share of the ECSC amounted to 42 percent; Japan, 13 percent; the United Kingdom, 6 percent; and the rest of the world, 11 percent. As mentioned earlier, the rise in imports from the rest of the world during 1966 was a new development, with significant quantities of steel originating in Poland, Czechoslovakia, and Australia.

In the Atlantic nations context, the significant change in the structure of Canadian steel imports has thus been a shift towards the ECSC and Japan, mainly at the expense of the United States, but also of the United Kingdom. Imports from other EFTA countries are not significant.

Canadian steel exports. Although Canadian steel exports[20] have been gradually built up in the postwar period, their volume remains modest in

[20]The figures shown here include carbon steel and alloy and stainless steel shipments. For alloys and stainless steels, Atlas Steels has developed a relatively large volume of exports in relation to total mill shipments, though the absolute numbers are, of course, small by comparison with carbon steel volumes.

TABLE 49

GEOGRAPHICAL ORIGIN OF ROLLING-MILL-PRODUCT IMPORTS, CANADA, 1953–66
(volume figures in thousands of net tons)

	United States Tons (000)	United States Percent	ECSC Tons (000)	ECSC Percent	Japan Tons (000)	Japan Percent	United Kingdom Tons (000)	United Kingdom Percent	Other EFTA Tons (000)	Other EFTA Percent	Rest of world Tons (000)	Rest of world Percent	Total Tons (000)
1953	840	78.0	110	10.2	4	0.4	121	11.2	1	0.1	—	—	1,076
1954	629	80.4	72	9.2	3	0.4	78	10.0	—	—	—	—	782
1955	772	82.7	75	8.0	18	1.9	69	7.4	—	—	—	—	934
1956	1,150	72.4	243	15.3	22	1.4	163	10.3	10	0.6	10	0.7	1,588
1957	1,146	78.6	172	11.8	9	0.6	118	8.1	3	0.2	1	—	1,458
1958	883	80.0	129	11.7	18	1.6	74	6.7	—	—	—	—	1,105
1959	510	54.3	233	24.8	44	4.7	152	16.1	1	0.1	1	0.1	940
1960	519	60.5	155	18.1	42	4.9	140	16.3	1	0.1	—	—	858
1961	355	51.7	225	32.7	30	4.4	75	10.9	2	0.3	—	—	687
1962	269	44.1	215	35.2	43	7.0	57	9.3	3	0.5	23	3.8	610
1963	267	37.3	299	41.8	53	7.4	78	10.9	5	0.7	12	1.7	715
1964	651	48.2	449	33.3	88	6.5	139	10.3	9	0.7	14	1.0	1,350
1965	525	28.2	904	48.6	194	10.4	190	10.2	11	0.6	37	2.0	1,861
1966	347	27.8	524	42.0	164	13.1	76	6.1	(a)	(a)	137	11.0	1,248

Source: 1953–65: Compiled from Economic Commission for Europe, *Statistics of World Trade in Steel* (annually). 1966: DBS, *Trade of Canada, Imports*, Dec., 1966.
Note: The ECE import totals, by comparison to direct compilations from DBS data, generally reveal small differences.

TABLE 50

CANADIAN EXPORTS OF ROLLING MILL PRODUCTS, 1955–66

	Ratio of exports to total mill shipments		Thousands of net tons 1966
	Average 1955 to 1966	1966	
Semi-finished steel shapes	35.8	15.6	51
Heavy structural steel shapes	1.1	3.7	16
Rails	26.2	25.5	72
Track material	17.8	19.0	12
Bars	2.8	3.9	59
Wire rods	2.0	1.9	8
Flat hot-rolled products	7.6	8.0	168
Flat cold-rolled products	9.1	14.3	286
Total rolling mill products	9.4	9.4	673

Source: Algoma Supplement, Table 21.
Note: Details may not add to totals because of rounding.

relation to the total output of the Canadian steel industry. As a ratio of total Canadian shipments of rolling mill products, exports have averaged 9.4 percent since 1955, and 10.9 percent from 1962 to 1966. In 1967 the ratio was 12.5 percent (see Table 47). The buildup took place in specific product groups and against the background of rapidly growing domestic steel requirements.

By product groups, Canadian exports are distributed as shown in Table 50. Exports of semi-finished shapes show an artificially high ratio in the 1955 to 1966 averages (35.8 percent), partly because in a number of years there were movements of semi-finished steel to the United States for conversion purposes, which was re-imported as finished rolling mill products. These transactions occurred while there was an imbalance between raw steel and rolling mill facilities among some of the Canadian mills.

Exports of rails and track materials have, for a long time, been identified with the Sydney, Nova Scotia, plant formerly owned by Dosco. In absolute terms, the rail exports show wide fluctuations, from a low of 10,000 tons in 1959 to a high of 149,000 tons in 1963. As the world demand for rails has been declining, the volume and relative importance of rails exports relate to past rather than future prospects.[21] Similar considerations apply to track-material exports.

[21]Algoma's Sault Ste. Marie mill is the only other Canadian mill with rail rolling facilities.

In heavy structurals, bars, and wire rods, Canadian exports are small, both absolutely and in terms of total output of these products. In the heavy-flat-rolled-product group, the rising volume of hot-rolled sheet and strip exports from the late 1950s until about 1963 in part reflected shipments to the U.S. automotive industry, made under the Canadian-content arrangements that preceded the U.S.-Canada automotive products agreement.

Over and above this, the Ontario steel mills have built up an export market for this product group in the highly concentrated metal-fabricating markets of the Great Lakes states,[22] where they compete effectively for a share of the regional consumption by means of high quality, competitive prices, and prompt delivery. In proportion to total mill shipments, exports of hot-rolled sheets and strip averaged 17.0 percent from 1955 to 1966. By comparison, the ratio of plate (including, if any, skelp) to total mill shipments was 4.0, bringing the product-group average to 7.6 percent. In the 1966 tonnage totals, these shipments accounted for 25 percent of the total.

The rapid buildup of cold-rolled and coated sheet and strip exports from token levels in the mid-1950s to volumes approaching 250,000 tons in the mid-1960s reflects two underlying forces. The first was the rising demand for cold-rolled sheet and strip under Canadian-content arrangements with the automotive industry. Second, "coated" cold-rolled sheet and strip (i.e., tin-plate) exports have been developed on a relatively large scale by the two Canadian companies with production facilities. No longer reported as a separate export category, tin-plate shipments in 1966 were nevertheless by far the largest component of Class No. 445–99 (sheet and strip, steel, n.e.s.), showing total exports of 125,000 tons. In contrast to the other exports in the flat-rolled-product groups, shipments in this class were widely diffused—to a total of fifty-four countries, with only six of these taking more than 5,000 tons (including the United States, which purchased 14,000 tons).

Exports of galvanized sheet, virtually non-existent in the late 1950s, have recently been at a level of 60,000 tons per year, and more than 10 percent of total mill shipments. Galvanized sheet exports were built up partly as a result of Canadian-content requirements of the automotive industry before the automotive products agreement came into existence.

In total, flat-cold-rolled-product exports amounted to 286,000 tons in 1966, accounting for 42.5 percent of all Canadian exports.

As can be seen from Table 32, virtually all of Canada's exports to the Atlantic group are to the United States. The remainder of our exports (significantly influenced by tin plate shipments) were scattered widely among overseas countries.

[22]Including Ohio, Illinois, Indiana, Michigan, and Wisconsin.

Ton for ton,[23] Canadian trade in steel emerges with a gradually narrowing deficit. At the peak of the capital investment boom in 1956, imports exceeded exports by 1.4 million tons, or 25.9 percent of apparent rolling-mill-product consumption.[24]

During 1958 and 1959, imports exceeded exports by an average of 736,000 tons, or 15.9 percent of apparent steel consumption. In the years 1960–63, net imports totaled only 387,000 tons, or 1.9 percent of apparent consumption; and in one year, 1963, export tonnages actually exceeded imports by a small margin.

The sharp expansion in capital expenditures between 1964 and 1966 once again resulted in a rise of steel imports, which, in the face of a slightly lower volume of exports than in 1963, resulted in a deficit in steel trade averaging 811,000 tons in the years 1964 to 1966, or 10.4 percent of apparent steel consumption. Among individual years, the 1965 net deficit of 1.3 million tons (15.4 percent of consumption) was by far the largest; by 1966 this figure had declined to 575,000 tons, or 7.5 percent of apparent consumption, and in 1967 it amounted to 300,000 tons and 4.1 percent of apparent consumption.

[23]In dollars the results would be somewhat different.
[24]The volume of imports remained high in 1957, partly because large quantities of skelp imports were required for the construction of the Trans-Canada pipeline.

3. The Impact of Private and Public Commercial Policy on International Steel Trade: Trends and Prospects

Introduction

What conclusions can we draw from the steel industry's expansion among the Atlantic nations and the sharp increases in international steel trade in the last fifteen years? If the quantities of steel moving across international boundaries freely in intra-ECSC trade and intra-EFTA trade and still hampered by various obstacles in most of the other important flows are a criterion, the record is impressive. Not only has output risen sharply, but international trade has increased even faster. However, we have until now regarded the international flows in terms of physical quantities, and this of course is only part of the story. For the ECSC and Japan, the sharp buildup of exports is an important consideration in their balance of trade and payments positions. For the United States, the trends in international steel trade have meant the opposite. From a surplus in trade in steel-mill products amounting to $560 million in 1957, the turnabout produced a deficit of $908 million in 1966.[1] In the light of the U.S. balance of payments position, the deficit in steel trade has become a worrisome element influencing the country's outlook in trade policy.

Other considerations cast a shadow over the trade data. First, as the comparative financial data in chapter 1 suggest, the financial position of the steel industries in a number of overseas countries is not robust, certainly not by the standards of performance expected from North American private enterprise. The members of the ECSC, with the exception of the Netherlands (and, intermittently, Italy), show profitability ratios that are low by comparison with those of Canada and the United States. For the Belgian and French industries, recent years' results are at an unsustainably low level and clearly at the bottom of our comparisons. The profitability of the Japanese industry, about half-way in the ranking in Table 26, generally falls slightly below that of the United States and substantially below that of the Canadian group. Even after allowing for inconsistencies and pitfalls in

[1]U.S. Senate, Committee on Finance, *Steel Import Study*, p. 67.

making these comparisons, a stronger financial picture emerges for the North American (and especially the Canadian) industries, compared with overseas steel industries. Yet it is the latter that dominate world steel exports. Are these tendencies consistent with one another, or do they require reconciling?

A part of the answer to this question lies in the price terms under which international steel trade takes place. In the North American price comparisons of chapter 1, we had the assurance of uniform base prices, which, combined with the relevant extras, transportation costs and tariff duties (where applicable), could be worked out to delivered prices at various consuming points. In this context we saw a substantial decline in Canadian, relative to American, steel prices over the postwar period. In this chapter, we will bring offshore steel-pricing into the picture and suggest that an important variable in the commercial policies of the steel industries in the ECSC and Japan is adherence to a two-price system, divided into so-called home prices and prices for exports.

The direction of this analysis will take us into the area of dumping, a subject that has been catapulted into prominence as a result of the Kennedy round agreement. Other commercial-policy aspects that will be covered in this chapter are the tariffs, quotas, and other manifestations of national trade policy (such as tax factors) affecting world trade in steel. Finally, we will undertake the evaluations called for under the terms of reference of the Atlantic Economic Studies Program.

Offshore price trends and price policies

We have been able to discuss steel-price trends in the Canadian and U.S. industries in relatively precise terms, using base prices, extras, and estimates of the most economical form of transportation, but similar precision cannot be attained in our discussion of offshore steel prices.

The price information we have compiled relates to the ECSC member countries, Japan, and the United Kingdom. It is essentially of two types. The first set of prices are so-called "home" list prices published by the OECD and its predecessor, the OEEC.[2]

The Special Committee for Iron and Steel has repeatedly emphasized the

[2]The Organisation for Economic Co-operation and Development came into existence under a convention signed in Paris in December, 1960, by the member countries of the Organisation for European Economic Co-operation and by Canada and the United States. Japan joined the OECD in 1963. The organisations have published annual surveys on the iron and steel industry since the early 1950s, which are the work of the Special Committee for Iron and Steel.

analytical shortcomings of the ECSC home-price data. For example, the 1963 report states:

The ECSC rules relating to sales by alignment allow Community companies to grant rebates on their list prices for comparable transactions to an extent that allows them to align their delivered price on the price list of another company based on a different basing point. Community companies can also align on the real terms offered by companies outside the Community. The published list prices of the ECSC countries do not therefore reflect the prices actually charged, especially during a period of fierce competition. During most of 1963, under the pressure of abundant supply, not only did the Community steel works align on the delivered prices based on the lowest price lists, but they also aligned frequently on offers from third countries.[3]

HOME PRICES

For comparative purposes, we are showing compilations of the home-price data relating to merchant bars and hot-rolled sheets (similar information is published on joists, hoop and strip, wire rod, and heavy plate). Table 51 shows the home prices for merchant bars in West Germany, France, Belgium, the United Kingdom, the United States, and Canada, annually as of January 1 for the years 1956 to 1966. The quotations are shown both in absolute prices and in indexes based on 1956. The Canadian and U.S. price data are from the sources shown in Table 16; the other data are compilations of the OECD. All quotations are in U.S. dollars per metric ton (this is the basis on which the OECD data are reported), and we have adjusted the U.S. and Canadian base-price quotations accordingly.

As Table 51 shows, the ECSC producers, particularly France, show home list prices substantially below the North American base prices. In the late 1950s, the common practice in the ECSC countries was to realign prices to the lowest prevailing Community prices, which at the time were those of France. Since the price data in Table 51 are all expressed in U.S. dollars, exchange rate changes are incorporated. Thus the French devaluation of 1958, the revaluation of the German mark of 1961, and changes under Canada's floating exchange rate up to 1962 and devaluation in that year are all reflected in the prices.

In relative terms, comparing trends in the home prices among the countries shown in the tables during the period 1956 to 1966, Canadian price patterns compare favourably with those of most of the countries shown. Belgium, starting with the highest price (except Canada) in 1956, shows an absolute decline in the home price to $90 per metric ton at the beginning of 1966, and a decline of 13 percent in the ten-year period. By comparison, the Canadian

[3]OECD, Special Committee for Iron and Steel, *The Iron and Steel Industry in 1963, and Trends in 1964*, p. 71.

TABLE 51

HOME (BASE) STEEL PRICES FOR MERCHANT BARS, SELECTED COUNTRIES, 1956–66
(U.S. dollars per metric ton, and indexes 1956 = 100)

Year	United States $/metric ton	United States Index	Canada $/metric ton	Canada Index	West Germany $/metric ton	West Germany Index	Belgium $/metric ton	Belgium Index	France $/metric ton	France Index	United Kingdom $/metric ton	United Kingdom Index
1956	103	100	109	100	89	100	103	100	65	100	98	100
1957	112	109	118	108	95	106	105	102	89	104	107	110
1958	120	117	121	111	99	111	110	107	87	101	117	120
1959	125	122	123	113	99	111	90	87	74	86	116	119
1960	125	122	125	114	99	111	104	101	82	96	116	119
1961	125	122	119	109	99	111	102	99	89	104	116	119
1962	125	122	114	104	104	116	102	99	89	104	120	111
1963	126	123	111	101	104	116	95	92	97	113	119	121
1964	131	127	110	101	104	116	95	92	97	113	119	121
1965	131	127	111	102	104	116	96	93	97	113	119	121
1966	131	127	116	106	104	116	90	87	97	113	119	121

Sources: OEEC and OECD, Special Committee on Iron and Steel, *The Iron and Steel Industry* (annual).
Note: Prices are as of Jan. 1 of each year and have been rounded to nearest dollar. Indexes are computed from unrounded data.

base price for merchant bars increased by 6 percent during this time span, comparing favourably with increases of 13 percent for France, 16 percent for West Germany, 21 percent for the United Kingdom, and 27 percent for the United States.

The price trends for hot-rolled sheets (representative of the flat-rolled-product categories for which demand has been rising rapidly in the postwar period because of their usage in consumer durable-goods industries) are shown in Table 52. The Belgian home prices show a decline of 10 percent in the period 1956 to 1966. France is next with a 4 percent increase, followed by increases of 8 percent for West Germany, 11 percent for Canada, 22 percent for the United States, and 26 percent for the United Kingdom.

In absolute terms, the North American base prices for hot-rolled sheets are consistently below those quoted for offshore producers. For example, at the beginning of 1966 the Canadian base price was $106 per metric ton and that for the United States, $117 per metric ton, compared with prices for offshore producers ranging from $124 in Belgium to $139 in the United Kingdom. The Japanese price listed at that time was $144, highest of any reported in this group.

Although we emphasize that the home prices shown for offshore producers cannot be considered international transaction prices, a few theoretical observations are possible.

1. In relative terms, the deterioration in the competitiveness of U.S. steel since the mid-1950s stands out. The same can be said for prices in the United Kingdom, since for both products in both countries the rise has been between 20 and 30 percent.

2. For hot-rolled bars, relative price patterns in Canada compare favourably with those of every country except Belgium. In the case of hot-rolled sheets, the 11 percent increase in the Canadian price from 1956 to 1966 falls below that of the United States and the United Kingdom but is higher than the price changes reported by the continental producers.

3. If one were to take absolute price comparisons into account in order to determine the theoretical possibilities for international flows, the lower level of North American hot-rolled-sheet prices would simply rule out any form of offshore competition in this product in the North American market place. In the case of hot-rolled bars, the possibilities are more difficult to determine. For example, on the assumption of a cost of ocean shipment of $15 to $20 per ton (for further discussion see page 100 below) and taking into account the U.S. tariff (which was 10.5 percent prior to the Kennedy round agreement and will drop to 7 percent, TSUS Item 608.46), a flow of merchant bars still appears theoretically possible in terms of the 1966 reported home prices for Belgium and for France, which, with respective home prices of

TABLE 52

HOME (BASE) STEEL PRICES FOR HOT-ROLLED SHEETS, SELECTED COUNTRIES, 1956–66
(U.S. dollars per metric ton, and indexes 1956 = 100)

Year	United States $/metric ton	United States Index	Canada $/metric ton	Canada Index $U.S.	Canada Index $Can.	West Germany $/metric ton	West Germany Index	Belgium $/metric ton	Belgium Index	France $/metric ton	France Index	United Kingdom $/metric ton	United Kingdom Index
1956	95	100	95	100	100	123	100	137	100	119	100	111	100
1957	103	108	106	111	107	123	100	137	100	124	104	125	113
1958	109	114	112	118	116	135	110	145	106	119	100	137	124
1959	112	118	114	120	116	135	110	145	106	103	86	134	121
1960	112	118	116	122	116	133	108	145	106	103	96	131	119
1961	112	118	110	115	115	133	108	145	106	119	100	131	119
1962	112	118	105	110	115	133	108	145	106	119	100	132	120
1963	112	118	101	107	115	133	108	135	99	125	104	141	127
1964	117	122	101	106	115	133	108	112	82	125	104	139	126
1965	117	122	102	107	115	133	108	124	90	125	104	139	126
1966	117	122	106	111	120	133	108	124	90	125	104	139	126

Notes and Sources: See Table 51.

$90 and $97, would be $41 and $34 below the corresponding U.S. base prices. The same conclusion does not stand up for imports into Canada. The Canadian base price is $26 higher than the Belgian and $19 above the French; and with a duty of 10 percent (Item 37900-1) and any reasonable assumption about ocean freight costs, imports would be ruled out.

These comments are entirely theoretical, since a set of other prices, referring to export transactions, exists, and it is to these that we now turn our attention.

EXPORT PRICES

To develop price criteria more meaningful to a measurement of price trends in actual international transactions, we have analyzed export prices published by the OECD and the Economic Commission for Europe.[4] These prices are based on market information; and although they often relate to special transactions of a marginal character, they are believed to be reasonably representative for a valid indication of export-price trends.[5]

Tables 53 to 55 summarize export- and home-price data for merchant bars, heavy plate, and cold reduced sheets compiled from the annual steel industry surveys of the OECD and ECE.

(*a*) *Hot-Rolled Merchant Bars.* For the price data on hot-rolled merchant bars, the following evidence emerges.

For the ECSC, the existence of a two-price system is documented. Since 1963, export prices have been below the lowest published domestic price of the largest producers in the ECSC. Prior to that, export prices exceeded the home-price ranges of the producers in 1957, 1959, and 1960 (years in which the steel-supply situation on the continent was still relatively tight). In 1958 and 1962, export prices were about mid-range of domestic price quotations and, in 1961, near the upper limit.

The volatility of export prices is considerably greater than is indicated by the annual January quotations in the table. Prices can change several times during the year and have substantially more flexibility than home-market prices. Export prices are sensitive to changes in world steel demand and supply conditions and trace a clear downward trend in the last decade (see figure 4), which was only temporarily interrupted in the spring of 1959 and in 1964.

In discussing the steel situation in Europe in 1959 and, more generally, the concepts involved in home and export prices, the OEEC Special Committee for Iron and Steel made the following observations:

[4]The original publication source for these prices is *Metal Bulletin*, London.
[5]OECD, *The Iron and Steel Industry in 1962*, Table 44.

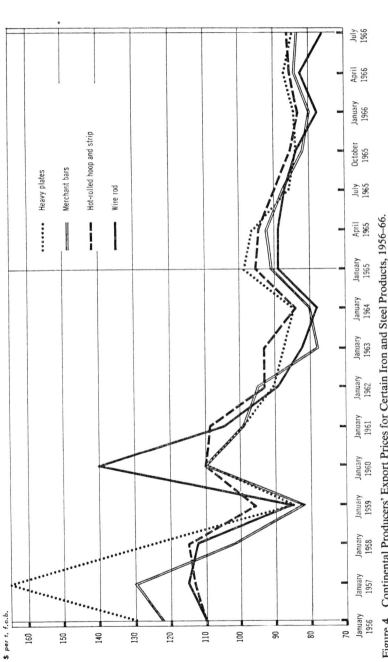

Figure 4 Continental Producers' Export Prices for Certain Iron and Steel Products, 1956–66.
Source: OECD, *The Iron and Steel Industry, 1966.*

TABLE 53

HOME AND EXPORT PRICES, MERCHANT BARS, SELECTED COUNTRIES, 1956–66
(U.S. dollars per metric ton)

Year	ECSC Export—f.o.b. Antwerp	ECSC Range of home prices	Japan Export	Japan Home	United Kingdom Export	United Kingdom Home	United States Export—f.o.b. Atlantic port	United States Base Pittsburgh	Canada Base Hamilton
1956	130	86–103				98		103	109
1957	95	89–105			124	107		112	118
1958	81	86–110	105	122	124	117		120	121
1959	110	74–99	93	103	112	116		125	123
1960	101	82–104	113	117	115	116	134	125	125
1961	95	89–102	100	111	115	117	134	125	119
1962	81	89–104	92	111	115	119	134	125	114
1963	84	95–104	80	108	115	119	134	126	111
1964	95	95–104	89	108	115	119	140	131	111
1965	81	96–104	100	108	115	119	140	131	110
1966		90–104	88	108		119	140	131	116

Sources: Economic Commission for Europe and Organisation for Economic Co-operation and Development for all prices of offshore producers and for U.S. export prices; Table 16 for U.S. and Canadian base prices.

TABLE 54

HOME AND EXPORT PRICES, STEEL PLATE, SELECTED COUNTRIES, 1956–66

(U.S. dollars per metric ton)

Year	ECSC Export—f.o.b. Antwerp	ECSC Range of home prices	Japan Export	Japan Home	United Kingdom Export	United Kingdom Home	United States Export—f.o.b. Atlantic port	United States Base Pittsburgh	Canada Base Hamilton
1956	165	98–117				91		99	109
1957	120	104–122				107		107	121
1958	81	109–130	220		162	117		112	122
1959	110	87–107	150	128	162	116		117	125
1960	100	97–107	115	144	116	113		117	126
1961	91	103–108	120	133	116	111		117	121
1962	90	103–122	113	133	116	112		117	115
1963	92	95–112	107	128	115	116	119	117	112
1964	100	95–112	115	128	115	116	119	122	111
1965	84	102–112	115	128	115	116	124	122	112
1966		89–112	110	128	119	117	124	122	112

Sources: See Table 53.

TABLE 55

HOME AND EXPORT PRICES, COLD REDUCED SHEETS, SELECTED COUNTRIES, 1956–66

(U.S. dollars per metric ton)

Year	ECSC Export—f.o.b. Antwerp	ECSC Range of home prices	Japan Export	Japan Home	United Kingdom Export	United Kingdom Home	United States Export—f.o.b. Atlantic port	United States Base Pittsburgh	Canada Base Hamilton
1956	156		206		138				116
1957	156	117–153	167		148			117	139
1958	138	117–153	146		146			127	142
1959	190	130–154	159		146	143		133	145
1960	150	135–154	152		146	140	140	138	147
1961	120	135–154	129		132	137	140	138	141
1962	115	142–154	129		132	137	140	138	134
1963	130	142–154	129	164	132	139	146	138	130
1964	114	142–154	129	157	132	147	146	144	130
1965	104		129	157		147	146	144	130
1966				157		146	146	144	135

Sources: See Table 53.

... export prices were again more flexible than home prices from July 1958 to the end of 1959. They had fallen in general, earlier than home prices when demand began to show signs of weakness; they were still falling in the last quarter of 1958 when home prices had become stable, but they began to rise somewhat before home price quotations.

The figures seem to suggest that there is a fundamental difference in the export price policy pursued by producers in the various exporting areas. Some, like the producers in the ECSC and Japan, seem to adopt a much more flexible policy than others, such as those in the United Kingdom and the United States. Although most steel producers agree that price changes have relatively little effect on total steel consumption in a given market, producers in the ECSC and Austria and those in Japan nevertheless seem to be prepared to try to expand their share of the export market by making price sacrifices in order to keep their plant in operation. This policy is in marked contrast to that followed in the United States, and, it would seem, in the United Kingdom, where the steel industries seem less disposed to offer heavy cuts in prices to overseas consumers. Producers in these countries rely to a lesser extent on exports and are, therefore, less readily influenced by conditions on the export market than producers in the ECSC, Austria, and Japan, who export a consistently higher proportion of their output. This difference in policy is particularly apparent in a period of recession.[6]

Before we can arrive at any conclusions on the penetration possibilities of ECSC steel into North American markets, two items must be added to the f.o.b. Antwerp prices: tariffs and ocean freight costs. The tariff would be between $8 and $9 (U.S.) per metric ton in recent years. The statistics on ocean freight rates are less readily accessible. The rates themselves are known to be highly volatile; published rates ("Conference" rates) typically are in a range from $15 to $20 per metric ton from western European ports to U.S. North Atlantic ports and from Japan to Pacific ports.[7] More applicable to ocean movements of steel would be tramp or charter rates; these are highly volatile but also lower than the published Shipping Conference rates, and can range from $5 to $20 per ton of steel. Combined with the tariff, a spread between ECSC export prices and North American base prices of $15 to $25 (U.S.) per metric ton would thus be required for possible imports into North American ports with production facilities.

With this as a background, the comparison of ECSC export prices and North American base prices theoretically explains the rising penetration of European steel into the U.S. market. In the Canadian-ECSC comparisons, the possibility is less clear-cut, though on the basis of figures for January, 1966, the $35-per-ton differential is theoretically large enough.

Japanese export prices also show flexibility and a downward trend, and the

[6]OEEC, *The Iron and Steel Industry in Europe, 1958 to 1959*, pp. 95–7.
[7]For example, see *Steel Import Study*, pp. 415–17. The periodic price compilations in *American Metal Market* also take into account ocean freight rates in their European continental steel-price compilations. (For example, on Jan. 9, 1968, a freight rate between $17.50 and $19.50 per metric ton is reported.)

comparison of home prices and export prices is again evidence of a two-price system. The conclusions as to possibilities for exports to the United States are similar to those for exports to the ECSC. For Canada, competition with the integrated Eastern producers becomes clearly possible at Vancouver, in view of the latter's overland freight costs.[8]

U.S. export-price quotations are $8 to $9 per ton above base prices. The export-price quotations of the American producers are f.o.b. Atlantic ports and include extra packaging costs, inland transportation costs, and loading. Reported U.S. export prices are thus in essence port-delivered base prices. The pricing policy here is opposite to that followed by the ECSC and Japan; there is a consistent spread above the domestic base price and no indication of price flexibility.

U.K. quotations indicate a small differential between export and home prices, with the export price slightly below the home price. Both quotations are relatively rigid over a long period of time and show no indication of price flexibility, either upward or downward. As to the level of prices, the British prices are intermediate between the export-price quotations of the ECSC and Japan and the higher North American base prices.

Canadian quotations are Hamilton base prices; no separate export price is published. Fluctuations in the base price since 1959 reflect exchange rate movements and, in early 1966, an increase of $5 per ton. The level of the Canadian price suggests that the only export possibilities would be to the United States.

(b) *Steel Plate* (heavy plate, ⅜" thick or more). The price data compiled for steel plate are summarized in Table 54. With few exceptions, the data lead to the same conclusions as for merchant bars. Export prices again show a high degree of flexibility in the quotations of the ECSC and Japan, compared to North American and U.K. prices. As one would expect, the direction of movement generally compares with that of merchant bars.

Among the special items to be noted in the steel-plate price data is a smaller U.S. differential between the base price and export prices ($2 per metric ton). Also, since the Canadian base price for plate has not been changed since 1957, all the fluctuations shown in the table represent exchange rate fluctuations. The relative movement of Canadian-U.S. prices affords an interesting example. The U.S. base price at the beginning of 1958 was $112 per metric ton, and the Canadian base price was $122 per metric ton. At the beginning of 1966, the situation was exactly reversed, as a result of two reinforcing movements: two U.S. base-price increases and the depreciation of the Canadian dollar.

[8]This may not hold in the case of merchant bars, for which regional production facilities exist. But it applies to our plate and cold-reduced-sheets examples.

For the United States, the possible penetration of ECSC plate into port destinations is clear-cut, though this does not hold for Japanese export prices. For Canada a number of distinctions must be made. At Toronto, the most recent level of ECSC export prices—$84 U.S. per metric ton in January, 1966, and $28 per ton below the Hamilton base price—would have theoretically created a price differential large enough to make shipments possible, if one assumes combined transport and tariff costs of approximately $25 per metric ton. The same conclusion does not hold for earlier price differences, which were in a range of $12 to $22 per ton.

Consequently, according to these most recent comparisons, the possibilities for plate-import penetration are even greater at Montreal and other eastern Canadian ports, since the Canadian delivered prices at these destinations would have to include freight from either Hamilton or Sault Ste. Marie.

(c) *Cold Reduced Sheets.* Comparative price data for cold reduced sheets shown in Table 55 point to the following conclusions.

ECSC export prices remained above the range of home prices until 1961 (except during 1958) and dropped sharply thereafter, falling from $150 per metric ton in January, 1961, to $104 per metric ton five years later, a period during which domestic prices of the leading producing countries remained virtually unchanged in a range of $135 to $154 per metric ton in 1961, as compared to a range of $142 to $154 per metric ton in 1966. For this product, U.K. data show stronger evidence of a two-price system, changing from higher export than home prices prior to 1962 to an opposite situation since then.

U.S. base prices increased from $117 per metric ton in January, 1956, to $144 per metric ton in January, 1966 (a price increase in December, 1967, brought the base price to $147 per metric ton). Even with this increase in domestic prices, the level of cold-rolled-sheet prices in the United States remained somewhat below the home prices reported by the ECSC's largest producers and Japan.

At the reported export prices, ECSC exports to the United States do not appear to have been feasible until 1963, but the declines in export prices during recent years now establish that possibility.

Japanese home prices (published by the OECD and the ECE since 1962) have remained considerably above U.S. prices; and even export prices, which were $129 per metric ton in 1965 (and $28 per ton below home prices), would not have had sufficient margin for Japanese exports to the United States.

Canadian base prices were above U.S. base prices until 1961, and since then the situation has reversed, although the base-price spread in the latest comparison still remains relatively small ($8 per metric ton). In terms of the export prices shown, this would preclude Japanese shipments; but the recent sharp declines in ECSC export prices again open doors for such shipments at their comparative 1966 levels.

Some of the preliminary findings of a study by the National Bureau of Economic Research (NBER) on international price competitiveness were mentioned in chapter 1. These findings are also based on concepts of export prices, but the Bureau's data collection has gone to original sources rather than the export prices reported in the *Metal Bulletin* and *American Metal Market*.[9] On the methodology of price comparisons involved, the NBER study found that its international price indexes for the United States until 1963 "followed very closely those computed from published export prices."[10] In 1963–64 a sudden reversal occurred, as the Bureau's indexes rose substantially, while those based on published prices rose only slightly. The Bureau suggests that this may be a sampling aberration or, more important, that "the index based on list prices published in the trade journals may understate the flexibility of American prices."[11]

Turning to ECSC export prices, the Bureau found that the published prices in *Metal Bulletin* are more volatile than those it collected,[12] giving the index of U.S. price competitiveness a magnified version of the fluctuations shown in the NBER index.[13]

On the subject of indexes based on home prices, the Bureau concluded:

From 1953 to 1957, U.S. domestic prices increased more rapidly than did the NBER international price indexes. Between 1957 and 1963, the two indexes moved quite similarly, and from 1963 to 1964 the international price index rose relative to domestic prices. As might be expected, European international prices diverged more frequently and by greater amounts from domestic prices, falling relatively in most cases in each of the periods between 1957 and 1963, and then rising by 10 per cent or more relative to domestic prices in both the U.K. and EEC countries in 1963–64.

It is clear that quite different conclusions regarding the last seven years' developments could be drawn from the domestic price data. Between 1957 and 1962, they suggest a much smaller decline in U.S. price competitiveness than is described by the NBER indexes, and between 1961 and 1962 they show an improvement while the NBER indexes show a worsening of the U.S. competitive position. In 1963–64 the comparisons based on domestic prices indicate a

[9]Kravis and others, "Measuring International Price Competitiveness, A Preliminary Report," NBER *Occasional Paper 94*, 1965, pp. 23–4 and 29–30.
[10]*Ibid.*, p. 29.
[11]*Ibid.*, p. 31.
[12]One reason for this may be the smaller product coverage.
[13]Kravis and others, "Measuring International Price Competitiveness," pp. 32–3. The competitive price deterioration of the United States vis-à-vis the EEC countries over the whole span of years: 23 percent instead of the NBER estimate of 4 percent since 1953, and 21 percent instead of 9 percent since 1957.

deterioration in the U.S. position and the NBER series suggest a turn toward improvement.[14]

The quotation on page 46, based on a later paper by two of the NBER authors, has already indicated their conclusions with respect to the deterioration of U.S. international competitiveness from 1953–63. The partial recovery in 1964, as the data on ECSC export prices indicate (see figure 3), will turn out to have been attributable to the temporary, but relatively sharp rise in ECSC export prices.

It remains for us to suggest the implications of price trends since 1964. On the evidence of the published export prices of selected products, sharp offshore price declines have occurred since early 1965; and in the face of U.S. price increases in each of the major product groups since 1964 (see Table 16), the conclusion that the U.S. competitive position declined substantially further after 1964 is inescapable. The sharp rise in U.S. imports from the ECSC and Japan supports this view.

Since we have not developed a full weighting scheme summarizing all trade in rolling mill products for the Canadian data, our observations for Canada rest on facts developed on a product-by-product basis. The figures for the selected products shown in Tables 53 to 55 support the view that the sharp declines of recent years in ECSC and Japanese export prices have widened the difference between offshore export prices and Canadian prices sufficiently to theoretically permit flows of ECSC steel to eastern Canadian markets and Japanese steel into Vancouver.

Dumping

Our assessment of the unfolding world price patterns is not intended to terminate with a rationalization of the flows in international steel trade that have emerged in the 1960s. An issue raised by the comparative price data of the large offshore exporters is that of geographic price discrimination implied in the differences between home and export prices. This is not only a matter of ready reference in many of the OECD and EEC reports, but is also implied in the evidence compiled by the NBER.

This takes us directly to a key issue in the current international steel-trade situation, an issue that is particularly important for Canada in the light of the negotiated Kennedy-round international code on anti-dumping policies. The code is designed to assure that "anti-dumping practices should not constitute an unjustifiable impediment to international trade and that anti-dumping duties may be applied against dumping only if such dumping causes or

[14]*Ibid.*, pp. 33–4.

threatens material injury to an established industry or materially retards the establishment of an industry. . . ."[15]

Canadian participation in the new agreement requires removal of the so-called automatic anti-dumping provisions, existing with various modifications since 1904, which provide that all sales of imported goods (of a class or kind made in Canada) at prices less than fair market value constitute dumping. The new Canadian law will require—along with the proof of dumping (i.e., lower export prices than home prices) that the previous law required—a fundamental change: proof of material injury or threatened injury to a domestic industry. Although this has been viewed with concern by spokesmen in a number of industries, the application of the existing law has in practice also not been automatic:

> It might seem . . . that the existing Canadian dumping law is too strong to be fully consistent with Canada's international obligations. This is, however, not the case. The dumping provision has always been a difficult one to administer, and those responsible for the day-to-day application of the law have usually had to rely to a considerable extent on complaints by domestic producers to pinpoint cases of dumping. This has meant that in practice the application of the dumping provision has in large part depended upon an apparent injury or threat of injury. Thus the Canadian law as actually applied is much closer to the spirit of the GATT provisions than the language of the Customs Tariff might suggest.[16]

Economic theory regards dumping as a type of price discrimination that constitutes a special problem in international trade; there is agreement on this point in the literature, ranging from Viner's 1923 classic on the subject of dumping[17] to current writers.[18]

In addition, dumping in steel trade has historical precedent; and in the light of the trends in steel trade emerging in the last decade, it is once again becoming a key element in non-tariff commercial policy.

The pressure of rising excess steel capacity has been increasing in the 1960s, and the global demand–supply situation does not suggest an improvement in the medium term. Under such conditions in past periods, steel showed itself highly susceptible to dumping, and the offshore price policies emerging in the 1960s suggest that history is repeating itself. Specifically applied to the Canadian steel market, the possibilities for dumping have increased because of recent years' sharp declines in ECSC and Japanese export prices. These

---

[15]Department of Trade and Commerce, "Agreement on Implementation of Article VI of the General Agreement on Tariffs and Trade" (mimeo.), 1967, p. 1.
[16]J. H. Young, *Canadian Commercial Policy*, Royal Commission on Canada's Economic Prospects, 1957, pp. 138–9.
[17]Jacob Viner, *Dumping: A Problem in International Trade*, Chicago, University of Chicago Press, 1923.
[18]See, for example, C. P. Kindleberger, *Foreign Trade and the National Economy*, New Haven, Conn., Yale University Press, 1962, p. 130.

have put the Canadian market within the reach of price-competitive imports. By comparison with the U.S. steel market, dumping in the Canadian market has been less of a market force until recently, but the requirements of the new anti-dumping code may alter this significantly because of difficulties in readily identifying home-market prices and in setting objective criteria for defining and proving "material injury."

Interestingly, the approach taken by the U.S. steel industry in its recent campaign to restrict steel imports has partially obscured the dumping question. Some of the allegations against imported steel have been about sales at or below the U.S. industry's cost of production[19] and about differences in wage costs. All this is irrelevant to the definition of dumping, which simply concerns itself with whether the export price is lower than the price in the exporting country. A rare published statement was made by C. W. Verity (president of Armco Steel Corporation) in a February, 1967, speech, in which he said that much of the imported steel is being sold in the United States for less than it sells for at home.[20]

In the battle mounted by the U.S. steel industry during 1966 and 1967 against imports, formal complaints against dumping were not publicized. In one instance, countervailing duties were imposed as a result of a complaint filed by nine U.S. steel companies with the Treasury Department against imports of structural steel from Italy, because export rebates were allowed on taxes not directly relating to the product.[21]

The major document emerging from the current steel-import debate, the steel-import study prepared for the Senate Finance Committee, has sidestepped the issue of dumping; and the massive outburst against imports that preceded it was not accompanied, as one might have expected, by an attack on dumping *per se*. It is interesting to speculate whether this resulted from the fact that the existing U.S. anti-dumping code requires proof of competitive injury to domestic producers, along with the evidence of price differentials.

In terms of future international steel-trading conditions, dumping remains a key unsettled issue. In an industry subject to large cyclical fluctuations and facing a high degree of demand inelasticity, dumping can persist long enough to cause the type of injury that the new code would seek to inhibit. The crucial element in the new code evolves around national definitions and measurements of injury to a domestic industry. But in the light of history this may be insufficient, as both the time horizon of the dumpers and their intentions are left out of consideration, and these are the real elements that the new Canadian code and its administration face.

---

[19]See, for example, *Wall Street Journal*, Dec. 20, 1967.
[20]*American Metal Market*, Feb. 23, 1967, pp. 1 and 17.
[21]*Journal of Commerce*, April 21, 1967.

Although not directly comparable (since in a Communist or socialist state it would be difficult to think of a market-price system, let alone a two-price system), the experience of the ECSC with the rise in steel shipments from eastern European countries during 1962 and 1963, at prices substantially below those prevailing in the ECSC markets, is interesting. When the price competition and the volume of sales aligned on offers from third countries increased substantially in this period, the High Authority of the ECSC moved, in early 1964, to stabilize the market by recommending the following:
1. An increase in existing external tariffs on steel imports, from their average of between 6 and 7 percent, to the Italian level of 9 percent.
2. The introduction of a special levy of $7 per ton on imported foundry pig iron, to be applied alongside the modified *ad valorem* duty at the present Italian level.
3. The interdiction to align ECSC works prices to iron and steel export offers made by the socialist countries of eastern Europe.
4. The maintenance and strengthening of quota restrictions on imports from the socialist countries of eastern Europe.[22]

These measures were initially limited in time, but they were first extended to the end of 1965 by the Council of Ministers and further extended at the beginning of 1966 by the High Authority and the respective governments because of uncertain trends in the steel industry in the ECSC countries.

Tariffs and the Kennedy round

THE TARIFF AS A FACTOR IN POSTWAR CANADIAN COMMERCIAL POLICY[23]
The main features of the Canadian steel tariff in the postwar period have been the several reductions negotiated under the GATT and a basic revision in the structure of the tariff in 1958, following lengthy hearings and a detailed study by the Tariff Board.

In the early postwar GATT conferences at Geneva (1947), Annecy (1949), and Torquay (1950 and 1951), some reductions were made in the steel tariffs of various countries, but almost from the beginning steel became an element of international dissent, particularly between the French and the Americans. Most of the major product groups in the Canadian tariff on rolling mill products were reduced in the 1948 and 1951 agreements,

[22]Economic Commission for Europe, *The European Steel Market in 1964*, p. 81; and Organisation for Economic Co-operation and Development, *The Iron and Steel Industry in 1964*, p. 49.
[23]For the historical facts on the Canadian iron and steel tariffs, the author is indebted to an unpublished (1967) study by Mr. Kenneth J. W. Burns of The Algoma Steel Corporation.

with cuts ranging from 2.5 to 5 percentage points in the *ad valorem* duties and from between $1 and $2 in the specific duties. The tariff structure was so complicated that the rates of the early 1950s cannot be readily summarized. Among the *ad valorem* duties, the range of rates was typically between 15 and 22.5 percent, and the specific duties were in the range of $6 to $7 per ton.

The next major event in the history of the Canadian steel tariff occurred in July, 1954, when the Canadian primary iron and steel industry asked the federal government for a complete overhaul of the tariff structure for the following reasons:

1. The Canadian steel-tariff structure had remained unchanged since 1907 and needed a complete revision and modification.
2. As a result of price increases, many specific duties in the steel tariff were outdated.
3. The U.S. tariff was considerably more up to date, while the Canadian tariff now included steel terms no longer commonly used in North America.

Subsequently, the Minister of Finance instructed the Tariff Board to conduct hearings and an inquiry into the steel tariffs, and these took place during 1955 and 1956. The Tariff Board report[24] was issued in February, 1957,[25] and its recommendations became the basis for the first complete overhaul of the Canadian iron and steel tariff in fifty years.

The Tariff Board recommended a new steel terminology built around four basic product groups: plate, structurals, bars, and sheet and strip. It proposed identical rates of duty for the main tariff items: 5 percent British preferential, 10 percent MFN, and 20 percent general tariff rates. Although it did not generally alter the average of previously existing rates, it recommended elimination of special concessions to certain classes of users and the removal of many specific duties in the tariff.[26]

The Tariff Board report was implemented after approval by Parliament, in September, 1958, by the Department of National Revenue. Following this, the Canadian steel tariff underwent no further changes except as part of the general surcharges following the June, 1962, austerity program (the last of which were removed in February, 1963) and of a new numbering system introduced in 1965, which did not alter the tariff items or the rates of duty. Table 56 shows the tariff structure that emerged from Reference 118. As can be seen, rates on more highly processed products were set above those on the four basic product groups; but in the Board's thinking, the changes

---

[24]Tariff Board, *Basic Iron and Steel Products, Reference 118.*
[25]There was also a simultaneous inquiry and report on steel pipe, Tariff Board, *Reference 119.*
[26]Tariff Board, *Reference 118*, pp. 93–5.

TABLE 56

CANADIAN CUSTOMS-TARIFF ON PRINCIPAL IRON AND STEEL ITEMS AT JULY, 1967

(rates are dollars per net ton or percentage of value)

(figures in parenthesis are new rates following implementation of Kennedy round of GATT negotiations)

Item	Commodity—abbreviated designations	British preferential	Most favoured nation	General
37400-1	Pig iron	$1.50	$2.50 (free)	$2.50
37700-1	Ingots of iron and steel, n.o.p.	free	$3.00 (free)	$5.00
37705-1	Ingots, round, corrugated, weighing not less than 30,000 lbs.	free	free	5%
37800-1	Semi-finished: blooms, slabs, billets, sheet bars	free	5%	10%
37900-1	Bars or rods, hot-rolled	5%	5%	20%
37905-1	Bars or rods, cold-drawn	5%	15% (12½%)	25%
37910-1	Bars or rods, further processed	5%	15% (12½%)	25%
37915-1	Wire rods, to .375," for wire	free	$3.00	$5.00
37920-1	Wire rods, to .375," for fencing (temporary)	free	free	$5.00
38001-1	Structural shapes, n.o.p.	5%	10%	20%
38002-1	Wide flange beams, 10"-18," not made in Canada	free	$5.00	$20.00
38003-1	Heavy structurals, not made in Canada	free	free	10%
38004-1	Sash to casement sections	free	$7.00	$7.00
38100-1	Plate, n.o.p.	5%	10%	20%
38105-1	Plate, flanged or dished	5%	20% (15%)	30%
38110-1	Plate, fabricated or further processed	5%	15% (12½%)	25%
38201-1	Sheet or strip, hot-rolled	5%	10%	20%
38202-1	Sheet or strip, cold-rolled	5%	15% (12½%)	25%
38203-1	Tinplate	10%	15% (12½%)	25%
38204-1	Zinc plate	7½%	15% (12½%)	25%
38205-1	Sheet or strip, coated, n.o.p.	7½%	15% (12½%)	25%
38207-1	Sheet or strip, electrical, silicon content 0.75% or more	5%	12½%	25%
38225-1	Sheet or strip, electrical, silicon content 2.90% or more (temporary)	free	free	12½%
38400-1	Plate, sheet or strip, hot- or cold-rolled	free	7½%	12½%
38500-1	Sheet or strip, terne-coated	free	free	15%
38700-1	Rails	5%	10%	15%
38710-1	Tie plates, fish plates, splice bars, rail joints	$5.00	$7.00	20%
39000-1	Castings, of iron or steel, in the rough, n.o.p.	15%	17½% (15%)	$8.00
39101-1	Castings—ingot moulds	free	free	27½%
39102-1	Castings—moulds, n.o.p.	free	7½%	free

TABLE 56 (continued)

Item	Commodity—abbreviated designations	British preferential	Most favoured nation	General
39200-1	Forgings, of iron or steel, in any degree of manufacture, n.o.p.	17½% (15%)	22½% (17½%)	30%
43015-1	Wire nails over 1″ and wire roofing nails of all sizes	$ .85*	$1.00*	$1.50
43020-1	Cut nails	$ .30*	$ .45*	$ .50
43025-1	Wire nails less than 1″ and nails or tacks of all kinds	10%	22½% (17½%)	30%
43030-1	Railway spikes	20%	30% (17½%)	30%
43035-1	Spikes, n.o.p.	20%	30% (17½%)	30%
44603-1	Manufactures, etc., of iron or steel, n.o.p.	10%	22½% (17½%)	35%
"Schedule B"				
	Goods subject to drawbacks for home consumption			
97004-1	Steel when used in the manufacture of files		99%	
97005-1	Steel when used in the manufacture of cutlery		99%	
97006-1	Hot-rolled hexagon bars of iron or steel when used in the manufacture of cold-rolled or cold-drawn bars of iron or steel		60%	
97020-1	Galvanized wire netting of a class or kind not made in Canada when used in traps for the fisheries		99%	

Source: Government of Canada, Department of Finance.
*Per one hundred pounds.

were designed to assure that the rates would apply to all users of the same steel and would be effective, rather than nominal or paper, rates. The Board concluded:

In that respect, the new classifications reflect an earnest effort by the Board to reduce—and, so far as possible, to remove—the scores of special concessions to certain classes of users which have served for years to dilute the apparent protection shown in the tariff; they reflect, also, an equally earnest effort to reduce existing rates wherever possible, to increase existing rates wherever warranted, and in the doing to achieve a balancing of result that should mean serious injury to none and greater fairness of treatment to all.[27]

The results of the Kennedy round negotiations must be considered under two headings: (1) the changes in the tariff rates agreed upon, and (2) the changes in non-tariff factors, among which the international code on anti-dumping probably is the single most important change for Canada.

The rates in the Canadian iron and steel tariff shown in the bracketed figures in Table 56 will be established following Canadian implementation of the Kennedy round-GATT agreement. The principal features are:

1. The four basic rates of 10 percent (applicable to bars, structural shapes, plate, and hot-rolled sheet and strip) have not been altered. This differs from the lineal cuts made on most principal items in the iron and steel classification by a number of Canada's major competitors.

2. A number of the rates on more highly processed products have been reduced, generally from 15 percent to 12.5 percent, representing a reduction of 2.5 points and 17 percent.

3. A number of the substantially higher rates (17.5 percent on iron and steel castings, 20 percent on flanged or dished plates, 22.5 percent on iron and steel forgings, wire nails, and iron and steel manufactures, n.o.p., and 30 percent on railway spikes and spikes, n.o.p.) were also reduced, with the highest of these rates being cut by the largest margins. All the reductions except one (a cut of the British preferential tariff on iron and steel forgings from 17.5 to 15 percent) were made in the MFN rate.

Reactions to the proposed tariff changes have generally agreed that the above cuts will not represent a material reduction in the effective scale of the Canadian steel tariff.

U.S. Tariff. The major items in the iron and steel tariff of the United States, with changes introduced in the Kennedy round, and values of Canadian exports in 1966, are shown in Table 57. The 20 cents per ton specific duty on pig iron has been eliminated, and the tariff rates on ingots and semi-finished steel, other than alloys, were reduced to 6 percent from 8.5 percent on imports valued not over 5 cents per pound and from 10.5 percent on those

[27]*Ibid.,* p. 95.

valued over 5 cents per pound. Alloy, ingot, and semi-finished steel tariffs were reduced from 14.5 percent to 8 percent (plus, in each instance, the alloy duties).

The tariff on rolling mill products was reduced by from less than 1, to up to 5, percentage points. Also, a number of specific duties have been reduced, eliminated, or converted into *ad valorem* duties. For the two product groups with the largest Canadian exports, the tariff on plates and sheets of iron and steel, not pickled, not cold-rolled (TSUS Item 608.84), was reduced from 8 percent to 7.5 percent; in the tariff on plates and sheets, pickled or cold-rolled (TSUS Item 608.87), the specific duty of 0.1 cents per pound ($2 per ton) was removed, while leaving the *ad valorem* duty at 8 percent. For plates and sheets, coated, not alloyed (TSUS Item 608.95), the specific duty of 0.1 cents per pound was removed, while the *ad valorem* rate was raised from 8 percent to 9 percent. The reductions in the tariff on specialty steels were generally larger, with cuts from a range of 12 to 14 percent to between 10 to 12 percent.

An analysis prepared by a staff member for the United Steelworkers of America shows that U.S. import duties in the steel sector will be reduced by a weighted average of 12.8 percent in equal instalments over a period of five years beginning January 1, 1968, and that the total reduction will drop the weighted tariff rate from 7.44 percent in 1966 to 6.49 percent in 1972. The analysis concluded that "it is clear that the Kennedy round will have little effect upon steel imports. In most cases the tariff changes represent only a fraction of the normal price fluctuations occasioned by market conditions."[28]

The additional competitive advantage gained for Canadian steel in the U.S. market from these tariff cuts is relatively small but will reinforce the competitiveness of Canadian steel, existing even prior to the Kennedy round cuts, in large steel-consuming centres of the U.S. midwest.[29]

Nevertheless, in terms of the structure and the volume of North American steel trade, the relatively small tariff reductions of the Kennedy round will not have a profound influence. The Canadian position may have been enhanced slightly by the U.S. tariff reductions; this holds proportionately more for stainless steels and alloys than for carbon steel. By comparison, the competitive disadvantage shown in chapter 1 for U.S. steel in large Canadian consuming centres prior to the Kennedy round will not be materially improved by the reduction in the Canadian tariff. As before, the U.S.-to-Canada

[28]Memorandum by Meyer Bernstein to I. W. Abel and others, dated Aug. 10, 1967, published in *Steel Import Study*, pp. 309–14.
[29]The January, 1968, U.S. steel-price increase on cold-rolled sheets and strip has further improved this margin.

TABLE 57

U.S. IRON AND STEEL TARIFF

TSUS item	Product description	Present rate	Final rate	U.S. imports from Canada, 1966 ($000 U.S.)
607.15	Pig iron	20¢ per ton	Free	19,793
607.30	Ferro chromium	8.5%	4%	380
607.35	Ferro manganese not containing over 1% by weight of carbon	0.6¢ per lb. on manganese content + 4.5%	0.3¢ per lb. on manganese content + 2%	569
607.37	Ferro manganese containing over 4% by weight of carbon	0.625¢ per lb. on manganese content	0.3¢ per lb. on manganese content	494
607.50	Ferro silicon containing over 8% but not over 60% by weight of silicon	0.8¢ per lb. on silicon content	Free	811
607.57	Ferro silicon manganese	0.9375¢ per lb. on manganese content + 7.5%	0.46¢ per lb. on manganese content + 3.5%	320
607.80	"Other" ferro alloys	10%	5%	386
608.02	Sponge iron	62.5¢ per ton	Free	751
608.15	Ingots, blooms, billets, slabs, and sheet bars of iron or steel, not alloy, valued not over 5¢ per lb.	8.5%	6%	7,877
608.16	Ingots, blooms, billets, slabs, and sheet bars of iron or steel, not alloy, valued over 5¢ per lb.	10.5%	6%	946
608.18	Ingots, blooms, billets, slabs, sheet bars of alloy, iron or steel	14.5% + alloy duties	8% + alloy duties	23,102
608.27	Forgings of alloy steel	14.5% + alloy duties	8% + alloy duties	1,873
608.40	Concrete reinforcing bars of steel, not alloyed, valued not over 5¢ per lb.	8.5%	7.5%	1,003
608.41	Concrete reinforcing bars of steel, not alloyed, valued over 5¢ per lb.	12.5%	7.5%	101
608.46	Other bars of steel, not alloyed	10.5%	7%	2,366
608.52	Bars of alloy steel	14.5% + alloy duties	10.5% + alloy duties	2,978
608.61	Hollow drill steel not alloyed, over 8¢ per lb.	10.7%	7.5%	765
608.62	Hollow drill steel, alloyed	14.7% + alloy duties	9.5% + alloy duties	733
608.84	Plates and sheets of iron or steel, not pickled, not cold-rolled	8%	7.5%	15,122
608.85	Plates, sheets of iron or steel, alloyed, not pickled, not cold-rolled	12% + alloy duties	9.5% + alloy duties	401

TABLE 57 (continued)

TSUS item	Product description	Present rate	Final rate	U.S. imports from Canada, 1966 ($000 U.S.)
608.87	Plates and sheets, pickled or cold-rolled	0.1¢ per lb. + 8%	8%	15,404
608.88	Plates and sheets, pickled or cold-rolled alloy iron or steel	0.1¢ per lb. + 12% + alloy duties	10% + alloy duties	1,088
608.92	Tinplate and tin coated sheets	0.8¢ per lb.	8%	209
608.95	Plates and sheets, coated, not alloyed	0.1¢ per lb. + 8%	9%	6,033
609.07	Strip of iron or steel, alloyed, over 0.01'' but not over 0.05'' in thickness	12.5% + alloy duties	10.5% + alloy duties	188
609.08	Strip of iron or steel, alloyed, over 0.05'' in thickness	13.5% + alloy duties	11.5% + alloy duties	255
609.15	Plates, sheet, strip of alloyed iron or steel	13% + alloy duties	10% + alloy duties	114
609.45	Round wire alloy iron or steel	12.5% + alloy duties	10.5% + alloy duties	727
609.82	Angles, shapes, sections, alloy iron or steel	0.1¢/lb. + 4% + alloy duties	0.1¢/lb. + 2% + alloy duties	1,647
609.84	Angles, shapes and sections, drilled, punched, not alloyed	7.5%	6.5%	658
610.43	Pipes and tubes, alloyed	11.5% + alloy duties	11% + alloy duties	466
610.51	Hollow bars, alloyed	15.5% + alloy duties	13% + alloy duties	666
610.80	"Other" cast iron fittings	19%	11%	255

Source: Department of Trade and Commerce, *Foreign Trade*, 128, No. 1, July 1, 1967, pp. 19–21.

TABLE 58

STEEL TARIFFS OF THE ECSC-MFN RATES
(percentages)

Item (BTN)[a]		Old	New
73.07	Semi-finished steel (blooms, billets, etc.)	4	4
73.10	Bars	8–10	6–7
73.11	Angles, shapes, and sections	9	6
73.13	Plate and hot-rolled sheets	8	6–7

Source: Compiled from Etats-Membres de la CECA, Liste XL BIS, supplied by Department of Trade and Commerce.
[a]Brussels Tariff Nomenclature.

flow of steel will be in those few products (generally in a more advanced stage of processing) that are not made in Canada, or in temporary supplies to fill in for shortages.

ECSC Tariffs. The important changes in the common external tariff of the ECSC countries include those set forth in Table 58. The new steel tariff of the ECSC is in a range of 6 to 7 percent, compared with the 8 to 9 percent level to which it was raised in 1964 as the result of the High Authority's effort to stabilize the European steel market. The data on absolute and relative price trends shown on pages 92–103 do not suggest that Canada's export potential to the ECSC will be in any manner enhanced as a result of the cuts. Canada's exports to the ECSC have been nominal in recent years, reflecting either one-shot transactions or special arrangements.

Japan. Japan entered the Kennedy round negotiations with the highest level of steel tariff among the major producing nations. As Table 59 shows, Japan agreed on across-the-board reductions of 50 percent on major items in the steel tariff.

The result will be duties on pig iron, ingot, and semi-finished steel ranging from 5 to 6.25 percent and a 7.5 percent rate on rolling mill products. The 7.5 percent rolling-mill-product rate has brought Japanese tariffs into the range of the ECSC and the U.S. steel tariff, compared to which the Canadian tariff on most rolling mill products still remains higher at around 10 percent. An interesting feature in the new Japanese steel tariff is the common grouping of hot-rolled and cold-rolled items into a single tariff rate; both the Canadian and U.S. tariffs still differentiate this, with higher rates on cold-rolled steel.

In view of the prevailing unilateral flows in Japanese steel trade (see Tables 30 to 32), the above cuts may turn out to be largely ceremonial as far as the volume of imports is concerned.

United Kingdom. The MFN rates in the United Kingdom's iron and steel

TABLE 59

JAPAN'S TARIFF ON STEEL PRODUCTS

Item no.		General rate of duty (percentage of *ad valorem*)	New rate of duty
73.01	Pig iron, cast iron, and spiegeleisen, in pigs, blocks, lumps, and similar forms:		
	1. Pig iron and cast iron	10	5
	Charcoal pig iron and low-phosphorous pig iron and cast iron classified here.		
73.06	Puddled bars and pilings; ingots, blocks, lumps, and similar forms, of iron or steel:		
	1. Ingots	12.5	6.25
	2. Other	12.5	6.25
73.07	Blooms, billets, slabs, and sheet bar, of iron or steel; pieces roughly shaped by forging, of iron or steel:		
	1. Pieces roughly shaped by forging	12.5	6.25
	2. Other	12.5	6.25
73.08	Iron or steel coils for re-rolling	15	7.5
73.10	Bars and rods (including wire rod) of iron or steel, hot-rolled, forged, extruded, cold-formed or cold-finished; hollow mining drill steel:		
	1. Bars and rods	15	7.5
	2. Wire rods, in coils	15	7.5
73.12	Hoop and strip, of iron or steel, hot-rolled or cold-rolled	15	7.5
73.13	Sheets and plates, of iron or steel, hot-rolled or cold-rolled	15	7.5
73.17	Tubes and pipes, of cast iron	15	7.5
Ex 73.40	Other articles of iron or steel, other than endless conveyor belts in rolls	20	10
	Classified here are iron and steel castings in the rough state; forgings, in rough state.		

Source: Compilation supplied by Department of Trade and Commerce.

tariff were generally reduced by a lowering of either the specific duties or the *ad valorem* duty, with typical changes in the latter being in the range of 2 percentage points.[30]

Prior to the Kennedy round, the United Kingdom had no tariff duties on steel from Commonwealth and EFTA countries, and in this sense the reduction in MFN rates reduces the margin of preference for these two groups.

[30]Schedule 19 of the British Customs' Tariff.

The same holds for the position of British steel in the Canadian market; the 5 percent level for most of the major product groups in the Canadian British preferential tariff remains (see Table 56), and the relative British preference is reduced to the extent of the cuts shown in the MFN rates.

The tariff impediments to Canadian-British trade were small, even prior to the Kennedy round; but as we can see from the trade data, the volume of British-Canadian steel trade has not been growing in either direction over the longer run.

Other EFTA Countries. The reductions in the major items of the MFN tariff of Austria and Sweden are summarized in Table 60. Denmark did not have tariffs on rolling mill products before the Kennedy round. The Swiss rates, which are specific duties, were not appreciably lowered.

TABLE 60

STEEL TARIFFS OF AUSTRIA AND SWEDEN—MFN RATES
(percentages)

Item (BTN)ª		Austria		Sweden	
		Old	New	Old	New
73.07	Semi-finished steel	9–10	5–7	4	4
73.10	Bars	12–13	6–10	5–7	5–6
73.11	Angles, shapes, and sections	12–13	7–9	6–7	6
73.13	Plate and hot-rolled sheets	12–18	7–15	6–15	6

Sources: Compiled from tariff schedules provided by Department of Trade and Commerce, Ottawa.
ªBrussels Tariff Nomenclature

Conclusions on the Kennedy Round. The Kennedy round appears to have brought about a greater harmonization of tariff levels among the major producing countries. The general range of many countries' tariffs on rolling mill products is now between 6 and 8 percent *ad valorem*; in some instances, as in the Japanese tariff, this required a 50 percent reduction from previous levels. By comparison, the ECSC and U.S. reductions were smaller. However, they started from an absolute lower level of steel tariffs. The Canadian tariff, with 10 percent rates on the basic groups of rolling mill products, will be above those of the other large producing countries shown in our tables.

Since the tariff cuts will in most cases be phased in five steps over a period of four years, the immediate impact of the steel-tariff cuts will be relatively small, certainly by comparison with the other determinants in international trade movements, such as prices and transportation costs.

Non-tariff factors in commercial policy

Among the non-tariff policies designed to influence international trade, one may include devices such as special provisions for valuation and classification; delays in administering regulations; marking regulations; copyright, patent, and trademark provisions; and food, drug, and health regulations. Governments, with their purchases, can discriminate against imports and, by their tax policies (other than the tariff), can encourage exports or further deter imports. Writing some years ago on the Canadian-American "invisible tariff," Masson and Whitely stated:

> One of the most striking features . . . is the variety and complexity of the methods used by each country to keep out the other's goods. Tariffs are probably the principal barriers, but few people in either country appreciate the extent to which the tariffs of each country have been supplemented by other forms of protection. Indeed, for some industries, quantitative restrictions have had a much more severe impact on the flow of trade than tariffs.[31]

In the area of steel trade, the following tables summarize the taxes (other than the tariff) imposed on imports among the group of countries included in our survey, and their comparative impact on U.S. exports and imports of steel. The data were compiled for the Senate Finance Committee study, which concluded:

> The European steel markets have always been less open than the U.S. market because of higher costs of entry due principally to the so-called "border taxes", higher tariffs and other restrictions that reflect close co-operation between the industries and the governments of these countries. . . . The net effect of these charges is a significant increase in the cost of entry which must be borne by imported steel mill products before they can be sold in the markets of these respective countries.[32]

With respect to Japan the study stated:

> Japan discriminates against competitive imports through a system of import licenses and exchange controls. In addition, Japan has comprehensive buy-national requirements which act as an effective non-tariff trade barrier to imports. Duties are levied on a cost, insurance, and freight basis as opposed to the free on board customs valuation used by the United States. Based on the experience of an American steel company, the Japanese trading houses have indicated that the commission for handling imported steel ranges as high as 30 percent.[33]

As can be seen from Table 61, only the United States and Canada assess *ad valorem* duties on f.o.b. values, while the other countries use c.i.f. values. Assuming that ocean freight costs are in a range of 10 percent of the delivered

[31]Francis Masson and J. B. Whitely, *Barriers to Trade between Canada and the United States*, Montreal and Washington, Canadian-American Committee, 1960, p. 1.
[32]*Steel Import Study*, p. 51.
[33]*Ibid.*, p. 51.

TABLE 61

COST OF ENTRY COMPARISON OF DUTIES, TAXES, AND OTHER CHARGES (EXCLUDING FREIGHT, INSURANCE, HANDLING, ETC.) PER $100 OF PRODUCT

North America

	Canada	United States
Tariff	Percent on selling price in market of exporting country*	Specific duties or *ad valorem* duties on f.o.b. value
Sales tax	Percent on duty-paid value of all goods manufactured or produced in Canada or imported into Canada unless specifically exempted from the tax under the Excise Tax Act. The tax is not levied at the time of importation when goods are imported by manufacturers, wholesalers, or jobbers licensed to pay the sales tax at the time of the final sale of the goods by them. Many specified products and materials are exempt from the sales tax if consumed or expanded directly in the manufacture or production of goods	

Europe
European Free Trade Association

	United Kingdom	Norway	Sweden	Denmark	Austria	Portugal	Switzerland
Tariff	Specific or *ad valorem* (c.i.f.) duties	C.i.f value	C.i.f. value	C.i.f. value	C.i.f. value	Specific duties	Specific duties
Turnover tax		Percent on duty-paid value	Percent on duty-paid value	Percent on duty-paid value	Percent on duty-paid value		
Sales tax							Percent on cost, insurance and freight duty-paid value
Statistical tax							Percent on total customs charges
Transaction tax						Percent on duty-paid value	
Import licences						×	
Exchange controls						×	

TABLE 61 (continued)

European Economic Community

	France	Italy	West Germany	Belgium	Luxembourg	Netherlands
Tariff	C.i.f. value	C.i.f. value	C.i.f. value	C.i.f. value	C.i.f. value	C.i.f. value
Sales tax	25 percent on the duty-paid value	4 percent on duty-paid value				
Customs stamp tax	2 percent on duty alone					
Compensatory import tax		4.8 percent or 7.8 percent on duty-paid value				
Administrative fee	0.2 percent of total customs charges	0.5 percent on c.i.f.				
Turnover equalization tax			2 percent to 9.5 percent on duty-paid value		3 percent on duty- and tax-paid value	0 percent to 11 percent on duty-paid value
Transmission tax				7 percent to 19 percent on duty-paid value		
Import tax					3 percent on duty-paid value f.o.b. Luxembourg	

Asia

	Japan
Tariff	C.i.f. value
Import licences	×
Exchange controls	×

Source: U.S. Senate, *Steel Import Study*, pp. 315–16 and 326.

*F.o.b. point of shipment in country of export.

TABLE 62

COMPARISONS OF TARIFF DUTIES AND OTHER TAXES IMPOSED ON STEEL TRADE AMONG U.S. AND SELECTED ECSC MEMBERS (U.S. dollars)

Hot-rolled and cold-rolled sheets (carbon steel)

Charges	From the United States to					
	Belgium		France		West Germany	
	Hot-rolled sheets	Cold-rolled sheets	Hot-rolled sheets	Cold-rolled sheets	Hot-rolled sheets	Cold-rolled sheets
Duty (c.i.f. value)	5.72	11.23	10.30	11.23	10.30	11.23
Sales tax			31.21	30.91		
Stamp tax			.21	.23		
Turnover equalization tax					11.85	11.74
Transmission tax	8.41	8.65				
Total charges ex dock foreign port	14.13	19.88	41.72	42.37	22.15	22.97

Charges	To the United States from					
	Belgium		France		West Germany	
	Hot-rolled sheets	Cold-rolled sheets	Hot-rolled sheets	Cold-rolled sheets	Hot-rolled sheets	Cold-rolled sheets
Duty (f.o.b. value), total charges ex dock New York	8.00	9.91	8.00	9.91	8.00	9.91

TABLE 62 (continued)

Flat- and hot-rolled bars (carbon steel)

	From the United States to					
	Belgium		France		West Germany	
Charges	Plates	Hot-rolled bars	Plates	Hot-rolled bars	Plates	Hot-rolled bars
Duty (c.i.f. value)	5.77	10.16	10.39	10.16	10.39	10.16
Sales tax			31.47	30.74		
Stamp tax			.21	.20		
Turnover equalization tax					10.69	10.47
Transmission tax	8.48	8.62				
Total charges ex dock foreign port	14.25	18.78	42.07	41.10	21.08	20.63

	To the United States from					
	Belgium		France		West Germany	
Charges	Plates	Hot-rolled bars	Plates	Hot-rolled bars	Plates	Hot-rolled bars
Duty (f.o.b. value), total charges ex dock New York	8.00	7.00	8.00	7.00	8.00	7.00

Source: U.S. Senate, *Steel Import Study*, p. 317.

price of North American steel, the incidence of protection afforded to the Europeans and the Japanese increases proportionately as the result of their valuation basis on c.i.f. values. This, however, can be considered as an offset to the higher level of tariff rates that will exist in Canada (and to a lesser extent in the United States) after full implementation of the Kennedy round tariff cuts, compared with the ECSC and Japan.

The disparate impact on imports resulting from indirect taxes is not indicative of discrimination *per se*, as long as it serves to put foreign goods in the same tax position as those produced domestically. In this sense, the Canadian federal sales tax and the European turnover, value-added, or sales taxes represent a greater emphasis on indirect taxation, compared to the U.S. federal tax system, even though the end result, as seen in Table 62, places U.S. steel exports on a different footing by comparison with imports into the United States.

A more fundamental divergence in non-tariff commercial policy arises in the treatment of exports for tax purposes, as, under the GATT, rebates are permissible if the remissions are made on indirect taxes.

Table 63 summarizes the indirect tax remissions used at present by the ECSC and the United Kingdom on their steel exports.

In Japan, indirect tax remissions are not used, but generous depreciation allowances have been an incentive for the steel industry's expansion—too generous, according to the following conclusion:

Another controversial case is the generous special depreciation granted the iron and steel industry. This may have been a cause of over-investment in that industry in 1959–60. Since the end of 1961, there has been substantial excess capacity in iron and steel, and a strict cartel to curtail production and investment, in which the government has participated, has been in effect. It is conceivable that in other cases as well some discriminatory special tax provisions may have misdirected rather than improved resource allocation.[34]

These examples by no means exhaust non-tariff aspects of commercial policy. Other factors to be taken into account are:

1. A marked acceleration in the European steel industry merger movement, particularly in West Germany and France. The West German steel industry has also been regrouped into four regional marketing offices, which will allocate domestic and export orders among various members. These marketing offices also make profit-allocating decisions and, when necessary, will shut down certain mills to obtain higher degrees of capacity utilization.[35]

[34]*Foreign Tax Policies and Economic Growth*, a conference report of the National Bureau of Economic Research and the Brookings Institution, 1966, p. 89. The paper on Japan (pp. 39–90) was presented by Professor Ryutaro Komiya of the University of Tokyo.

[35]*Center Lines*, II, special supplement, March 1967, published by the Steel Service Center Institute. The special article on U.S. and foreign steel developments was pre-

125 TRENDS AND PROSPECTS

TABLE 63

INDIRECT TAX REMISSIONS EFFECTIVE ON STEEL EXPORTS
BY ECSC MEMBERS AND THE UNITED KINGDOM

	Value-added tax	Turnover tax (percentages)	Applicability to exports	Other features
Belgium		7	exempt	
France	25%		exempt	
Italy		4	exempt	4.8% refund of export price[a]
Luxembourg		3	exempt	1% refund of export price[a]
West Germany		4	exempt	0.5% to 4% of export price[a]
United Kingdom				2.75% to 3% rebate on f.o.b. export value

Source: Compiled from *Steel Import Study*, pp. 36–8
[a] To recover turnover taxes previously paid on materials purchased.

2. The encouragement given by the French government to the moderniza-
tion of steel-industry facilities by means of a low interest loan up to $600
million. When this amount is used up, an additional $900 million will be
available to the industry, with the ultimate objective of increasing French
steel production to 25 million metric tons per year.[36]
3. The "loyalty rebates" proposed by British Steel Corporation, which would
institute a $4 per ton rebate on sheets at the end of January, 1968, for
purchasers that have not used any foreign sheet steel within the previous six
months' period. This rebate would apply on all their domestic sheet purchases
during that time. This proposal evoked a U.S. complaint at the GATT
meeting of December 20, 1967.[37]
4. The extent to which government ownership and control exist in the steel
industries of various nations. This is a widespread phenomenon among the
relatively new steel industries of Latin American, Africa, the Middle East,
and the Far East. It is also found in a number of the ECSC and EFTA
countries, as the compilation in Table 64 shows.
   In the area of non-tariff commercial policy, the Kennedy round provided
only one major change. This was the new agreement on anti-dumping,
which, as we have shown above, holds important implications for Canada
in the light of the existing automatic anti-dumping provisions.[38]

pared by the Reverend William T. Hogan, s.j.
[36]*Ibid.*, p. 2.
[37]*American Metal Market*, Aug. 17, 1967, and Jan. 5, 1968.
[38]Another change was in the so-called "American-selling-price" package, under which
the American negotiators agreed to abolish the American selling price for chemicals in
exchange for the elimination of certain European road taxes which are based on engine
size. *Ibid.*, Jan. 15, 1968.

TABLE 64

GOVERNMENT OWNERSHIP AND CONTROL OF ATLANTIC NATIONS STEEL PRODUCERS

Country	Company	Latest annual raw steel production (net tons)	Percentage of national production	Degree of government control
ECSC				
West Germany	Salzgitter Huttenwerk A.G.	2,500,000	6	Government-owned
	Ilseder Hutte	1,100,000	3	State of Lower Saxony holds 25 percent interest
	Schwabische Huttenwerke GmbH.	—	—	State of Baden-Wurttemberg holds 50 percent interest
Italy	FINSIDER Group	8,100,000	58	Government (through Instituto per la Ricostruzione Industriale, I.R.I.) holds 54 percent interest
	Societa Nazionale per Azioni—(Cogne)	250,000	2	Government-owned, but not part of FINSIDER
	Stabilimenti di Sant' Eustacchio S.p.A.	—	—	Government holds 51 percent interest.
Netherlands	Koninklijke Nederlandsche Hoogovens en Staalfabrieken N.V.	3,100,000	89	Owned 40 percent by government and city of Amsterdam and 60 percent by private interests
EFTA				
Norway	A/S Norsk Jernverk	540,000	71	Government-owned
Portugal	Siderurgica Nacional	301,000	100	Government owns 15 percent
Sweden	Norrbottens Jarnverk Aktiebolag	550,000	11	Government has interests
United Kingdom	Richard Thomas & Baldwin, Ltd.	3,690,000	12	Government-owned
	Thirteen other companies re-nationalized June 28, 1967	23,350,000	76	Re-nationalized June 28, 1967
Austria	VOEST—Vereinigte Österreichische Eisen und Stahlwerke, A.G.	1,920,000	54	Government-owned
	Österreichisch-Alpine Montangesellschaft	1,060,000	30	Government-owned
	Steirische Gusstahlwerke, A.G.	—	—	Government-owned (controlled by Alpine-Montan)
	Karntnerische Eisen und Stahlwerke A.G.	—	—	Government-owned (controlled by Alpine-Montan)
	Gebr. Bohler & Co. Aktiengesellschaft	—	—	Government holds substantial interests

Source: *Steel Import Study*, pp. 305–7.

Not only were the questions of various indirect tax levies or remissions left unsolved at the GATT, but the U.S. position changed significantly early in 1968, when the Administration was reported considering (as part of its balance of payments deficit-reduction program) export rebates and a surtax on imports.[39] In the event of their adoption they would have significant reverberations in the steel-trading picture, even though it has been shown that there is ample precedence in the area of border taxes among other Atlantic nations. Admittedly, the campaign mounted by the steel industry during 1966 and 1967 to obtain additional protection in the form of either temporary tariff increases or import quotas reached a dead end in the light of the Administration's opposition to policies directly aimed at steel. But in a more general defensive program, adopted for balance of payments purposes, steel imports would definitely experience a part of the fallout.

Just how much uncertainty surrounds the steel-policy area is evidenced by the inconclusiveness of the Senate Finance Committee's *Steel Import Study*:

It is by no means clear, however, whether such specific recommendations as a temporary levy on imports or a rollback quota would, at this time, be in the best long-term interest of the country or even of the industry. However, some responsible, short-term measure along these lines may be the prod needed to cause the steel producing nations of the world to join together in an effort to solve problems of world steel in a manner calculated to serve the best interests of all of them.

The arguments against Government intervention to provide protection for the domestic industry are persuasive in the abstract. The goals of keeping political alliances, maintaining price stability, and pursuing a consistent trade policy that upholds the principle of comparative advantage are all worthwhile and important. The real question is, however, at what point can a nation afford to allow one of its vital industries to undergo a serious decay because of imports? Perhaps the United States could afford to import 10 percent of its domestic consumption of steel. But would it be in the national interest to import 15, 20, 30, or even 50 percent? It is the trend which must be of concern, and a judicial decision will have to be made at some point as to how much the Nation can depend on imports of steel to meet domestic civilian and defense needs.[40]

Conclusions

Viewed in the context both of domestic policies and of international trading relationships, the steel industries of the Atlantic nations (and elsewhere in the world) are at a major crossroads. Their basic choice now divides between pursuing policies accommodating the major steel-market trends of our times

[39]*Ibid.*, Jan. 10 and 15, 1968.
[40]*Steel Import Study*, pp. xxiv and 252.

or facing a further deterioration in the climate of world steel trade. The elements that a positive set of policies will have to consider in the medium-term future include the following:

1. A rising level of investment expenditures on new, cost-reducing technology. This tends to bring with it capacity expansion at a time when it may not be required and, given the price policies of the steel industries in most countries, tends to exert further pressure on steel markets.

2. The rates of growth in the demand for steel in many of the large producing nations have dampened. This, in turn, has tended to reduce not only output gains, but also cash flows and profitability, which, in the environment of earlier postwar periods, greatly assisted in the financing of investments. As a result, the financial commitments of the North American industries may, in the foreseeable future, again seek the guidance provided by reliance on market mechanisms. To the extent that offshore producers use methods that tend to undermine market mechanisms—and recent policy steps illustrate their resistance to abandoning such methods—further disparities in commercial policy and additional distortions in the structure of world steel trade are in the cards. The national policies toward steel—such as are seen developing increasingly in West Germany, France, and the United Kingdom —run counter to the terms of reference of this study, which are inclined to a liberalization of international trade.

3. Beyond the Atlantic nations' boundaries, many other steel industries have come into existence around the world, often built on national policies and invariably limiting the growth in the export potentials of the world's "traditional" steel exporters, who are virtually all in the Atlantic group. As a consequence, the working off of the excess capacity now existing will be slower and more difficult than would otherwise have been the case. Non-market pricing policies tend to encourage producers to keep old capacity as well as to create new capacity.

The range of possible solutions to these conditions can be viewed under the terms of reference of the Atlantic Economic Studies Program, which require the answers to two major questions:

1. How would the steel industries in the Atlantic nations respond to special sectoral arrangements either for liberalizing or for stabilizing international trading behaviour in their own sphere? In fact, would they be instrumental in originating them?

2. How would these steel industries adapt to more general schemes for freer trade, embracing other products as well as steel, in which the specific interests of steel industries might or might not be directly represented in any special way?

Since our analysis is basically from a Canadian vantage point, our answers are based on the Canadian industry's competitive position. Whichever way we may see things, it must be remembered that the Canadian industry and the Canadian steel markets are small by the standards of size among the Atlantic nations.

To answer these questions the following findings in our study are relevant:
1. The Canadian steel industry has matured, particularly since the mid-1950s, into a technologically advanced, efficient industry, capable of supplying virtually all of a small and, until recently, rapidly growing domestic steel market. In the process it has replaced imports (particularly from the United States) which formerly supplied a large share of the Canadian market and has built up a modest volume of exports. By the standards of productivity trends, rate of utilization of productive capacity, and profitability, the Canadian industry has achieved a high standing among the Atlantic nations' steel industries.

The rapid growth demanded from the steel industry in Canada in order for it to become the major source of supply of rising domestic steel demand has, until recently at least, obscured the intensive competition emerging in world steel markets as a result of over-expansion of steel-producing facilities among the world's leading steel producers. As Canada was largely a "deficit-importer" until the mid-1960s, its steel markets did not feel the full impact of price-competitive trade, evident first in the late 1950s, and much more strongly in the early 1960s, in U.S. steel markets.
2. The U.S. steel industry has tumbled from the position of pre-eminence it occupied in the early postwar years, losing both a substantial amount of the export markets it had in Canada and offshore and, more significantly, a rising portion of its domestic markets to imports, mostly from the ECSC countries and Japan.

The reasons for the loss of its competitive position appear to be reflected in the price competitiveness of offshore supplies and in the shifts in international trade. Yet, in the absence of reliable comparative international cost studies and in the face of the available financial performance yardsticks, one remains uneasy about where the strictly "economic" factors would properly locate the patterns of steel production and trade, even though the *de facto* criteria—share of world exports or share of supply of domestic steel requirements—show the loss of ground of the U.S. steel industry.

At the root of the American experience is the intensified competition in international steel markets, attributable to the emergence of substantial quantities of excess productive capacity in the world's steel industries. When the U.S. steel industry first experienced this in the late 1950s, its policy consisted in maintaining prices, sacrificing volume, and accepting reduced profit margins. This had a significant impact on the balance of steel trade and, eventually, unfavourable implications for the U.S. balance of payments position. By comparison, as the pressure of excess capacity spread to the ECSC, Japan, and smaller producing nations, it expressed itself in downward pressure on steel prices, particularly export prices.

Along the way in this decline, American steel has felt the impact of private and public commercial policies among offshore producers; many of these policies differ materially from the standards of competitive behaviour in North America. The attempts to emphasize non-tariff commercial policy at the Kennedy round negotiations and the 1967 revival of the domestic battle for additional protection are evidence of a significant hardening of U.S. attitudes. These raise the thought of a new outburst of non-tariff protectionism that could well change the Kennedy round thinking, which was designed to expand world trading volumes.

3. The establishment of the European Coal and Steel Community was the single most important step towards liberalizing steel trade in our times. But though the ECSC began with conspicuous achievements, it cannot be viewed as an unqualified success in the retrospect of fifteen years.

On the assumption that rational decisions are behind the huge tonnages now moving freely across the boundaries of the Six, the record of growth in their steel trade is impressive, even if we allow that there were substantial volumes of steel moving among the Six prior to the ECSC and that the western European reconstruction and boom years favoured growth in steel demand and steel trade in the formative years of the Community.

But the Community tonnages are deceptive on several counts, and their size should not overwhelm us. The planning mechanism of the members of the ECSC has proven fallible and unable to accommodate, without making significant investment errors, the changes in economic growth rates and steel demand in various countries, to say nothing of other world trends.

These miscalculations share the responsibility for the growing volume of excess productive capacity, the downward trend in export prices, and the unsatisfactory financial performance of most of the member countries' industries, with the exception of the Netherlands. Clearly, the prosperity of the western European steel industries has not been commensurate with their size, and recent-year policies of the High Authority and of individual governments among the Six (particularly France and West Germany) reflect these developments. One implication of these trends is that we can by no means be sure that, in the framework of Atlantic trade, the export gains of the ECSC are based on an international competitive advantage in steel production.

4. What about Japan? From our annals, Japan is a success story in steel in the postwar period, but its trading stance sets it apart from the rest of our

group. Except for sporadic deficit-covering imports, Japanese steel trade is essentially a one-way street involving a massive buildup of export markets. What differentiates Japan from the ECSC is the greater prosperity of its industry and the apparent long-term goal of building large steel-using export industries; this suggests that the emphasis on expansion of exports of steel rolling mill products may be an intermediate phase.

Nevertheless, one is left with nagging doubts about Japanese steel in the international picture. Until the Kennedy round, Japan's level of steel tariffs was the highest among the large steel powers; and this, combined with stand-by import licences and foreign exchange controls and interwoven corporate relationships between steel producers and major consumers, has precluded the access of foreign steel into Japanese markets. The available price data indicate the existence of a highly flexible, two-price system. How necessary is this in view of the evidence that Japan has built a technologically efficient steel industry?

5. Renationalized steel in Great Britain faces the task of internally re-organizing and streamlining its operations and reversing many of the postwar trends that have led to the decline in its international competitive position. It is difficult to state our expectations under such conditions. Structurally, we are now dealing with an almost completely state-run industry. Government participation also exists, to a lesser extent, in a number of other Atlantic countries (Austria, Italy, the Netherlands, Norway, and West Germany),[41] which means that the privately owned industries of the United States and Canada are structurally in a very different position.

6. In addition to the large Atlantic steel producers, there are many others who have started or have rapidly developed a domestic steel industry in the postwar period. In the Canadian, Australian, and a few other situations, this development came in response to economic conditions and was market-oriented. In many other instances, it resulted from national policy seeking the prestige of having a steel industry.

By the standards of size in the United States, the ECSC, Japan, or even the United Kingdom, these industries are relatively small. The steel industry of Canada or of the combined EFTA group excluding Britain is in each case at a 10-million-ton annual raw-steel-capacity level. By comparison with 174 million tons in the United States, 120 million tons in the ECSC, and 62 million tons in Japan, this is comparatively insignificant. But there are many other steel industries. In 1966, Argentina, Australia, Brazil, India, Mexico, Spain, the Union of South Africa, and Yugoslavia had steel industries producing more than one million tons of raw steel each, accounting for a combined total of more than 25 million tons, compared to 5 million tons

[41]See Table 64.

in 1950. Regardless of what their rationales might be, these and many other small industries have displaced imports (and, in some cases, become exporters of certain products), thus affecting the export potentials of the major Atlantic producers.

Nor can the Communist bloc's steel be left entirely out of our consideration—eastern European steel has shown up in the ECSC and, more recently, in Canada, and our terms of reference cannot readily cover this competition.

What have been the accompanying developments on the commercial-policy side in the steel world? The conclusion of the Kennedy round leaves us with steel tariffs among the major Atlantic nations that are largely ceremonial and increasingly insignificant in relation to the transport costs and the obligations of heavy fixed-capital commitments. The smaller producing countries (Canada included) still have MFN tariff rates above the level of the Big Three, but these are no longer a roadblock to the expansion of steel trade.

Similarly, the tariff cuts under the Kennedy round are not about to alter the main patterns of Atlantic steel trade (though they could, at the margin, increase the price-competitive trade pressures that are already evident). The reason for this, as experience in the postwar period clearly indicates, is that the gradual dismantling of steel tariffs is not permitted to express anything like its full potential towards determining the direction of international steel trade among the Atlantic nations or other countries. Steel, in many countries, is an important instrument of national policy—a means to prestige and to balance of trade improvement through import substitution or export promotion. The commitments are now too heavy and too fixed to allow the free play of the forces of comparative advantage, and individual national steel industries will be maintained as instruments of policy whether they are economically viable or not.

The main emphasis of commercial policy has, of course, swung to non-tariff issues—including dumping, border taxes, and export incentives. It is in these areas that there is substantial malaise in international steel markets, because the Kennedy round did not really solve any of the basic questions and because, in a cyclical industry such as steel, the new anti-dumping agreement, requiring definition of price differentials and proof of material injury to a domestic industry, may act to reinforce present trends—that is, to encourage dumping—rather than to arrest them. Whatever the benefits of the new anti-dumping code may be for international trade in general, it is unlikely that it will be helpful in settling current problems in international trade in steel.

Where does all this lead the major steel producers in terms of the moods of their commercial policies? Interpreted optimistically, the first International Iron and Steel Institute meeting in November, 1967, showed a new willingness on the part of the world's leading steel nations to sit down and recognize the competitive problems arising out of the existing excess productive capacity and to clarify the invisible elements that enter steel trade, including certain pricing and other competitive practices and certain national policies in the areas of taxation and trade. It is too early to speak of an eventual consensus on these matters, but the alternatives to a basic new agreement on non-tariff policies are not pleasant to contemplate. Such alternatives are evident in the actions taken in recent years by the ECSC and by some of its individual member governments to protect and promote their industries. Similarly, they are seen in the mounting pressure exercised by American steel interests for additional protection against rising steel imports.

Under these circumstances, the prospects for new types of special international arrangements for freer trade in steel depend primarily on whether the Atlantic nations' steel industries and governments can arrive at a settlement of major non-tariff commercial-policy issues in the near term.

The common-interest basis and the ground rules of an international agreement on non-tariff commercial policies are by no means easy to establish, even given the desire to negotiate. Among the Europeans, government ownership and government intervention in the affairs of steel are widespread. The Japanese negotiators represent private interests, but there is close cooperation and understanding between business and government. It is against such forces that the Canadian and American steel industries, privately controlled and basically not operating under any national policy for steel, would have to be matched. If still other nations appear at the bargaining table, one can be certain that they too will represent industries that are slated to be maintained in each national entity as a matter of national policy.

Irrespective of our findings relating to the development and apparent competitive strength of the Canadian primary iron and steel industry, the time does not appear ripe for Canada to consider specific sectoral arrangements for freer steel trade with offshore members of the Atlantic group. If one had the possibility of starting all over in building up (or not building up) various nations' steel industries or of now eliminating the dead weight of the past, the answer might be different. But there can be no question of this in the light of developments that have already taken place and of the entrenched position of steel in national government policy outside North America.

A broad look at Europe readily provides the answer. The ECSC steel industries dominate the European picture, and at some future time the Community may be asked to absorb some or all of the EFTA group, in which the British, Austrian, and Swedish steel industries would be the main factors. If these developments occur, they will be largely dictated by political and general economic objectives of further European integration.

From the standpoint of these overseas steel industries, there is no apparent room for including the Canadian steel industry in such a scheme of things. Moreover, we can argue convincingly that our relatively small but prosperous industry would not find itself comfortable in the environment of European steel. A Canadian approach designed to augment the two-way flow of steel with the Europeans would basically clash with the increasingly inward-looking attitude of the ECSC and the stance of a nationalized industry in the United Kingdom. Nor does a greater rapprochement with the other EFTA countries appear to be in the cards; the channels of steel trade of the group are already largely European and will tend to become increasingly so in the future.

Similarly, the trading stance of Japanese steel does not appear conducive to exploring possible extensions of two-way steel trade. Economic geography is helpful to Japanese steel in Canada's West Coast markets, and the St. Lawrence Seaway has extended the seafaring steel trade of Japan in mid-western U.S. and eastern Canadian ports. Free trade in steel would reinforce this position, but in the light of Japanese competitive practices and commercial policy towards steel, it would remain a one-way avenue. The unanswered question in regard to Japan, even more so than in regard to Europe, is the degree to which it would be competitive in a setting adhering to North American rules of competitive behaviour.

The obstacles to thinking about trading relationships in steel among countries that are geographically widely spread arise from fundamental industry characteristics. Steel must be differentiated from other industries not only in terms of its capital intensiveness, cyclical volatility, and demand inelasticity, but also because of relatively high transport costs in relation to final market price. Several other structural factors come into play. First, individual steel industries normally develop into supplying the full range of rolling mill products and, in doing so, eliminate the possibilities of international intra-steel-industry specialization. Secondly, to remain internationally competitive has required the utilization of cost-reducing technology dependent on large volumes of investment, accompanied by more-rapid increases in capacity than would be dictated by demand trends. Thirdly, while there have been merger waves on the continent of Europe and while there is evidence of some reaching out of the American steel industry beyond its national borders, steel basically remains a domestic industry in most countries. Viewed across either the Atlantic or the Pacific, these structural characteristics are not an aid to specific sectoral agreements.

Although these conclusions do not support policies designed to tie the Canadian industry closer to the steel industries of the offshore Atlantic nations, they point to the areas in which harmonization and better understanding are absolutely necessary. It appears necessary that the governments of the world's major steel-trading nations should take an interest in arriving at special sectoral arrangements in international trade in steel. Even though these would be unlikely to lead us in the direction of free trade, they might be a stabilizing and rationalizing influence over the events that have taken place in the last decade. They might also relieve North American steel markets from bearing the full brunt of the offshore producers' two-price system.

How would the Canadian steel industry fare in such a scheme of things? Whether viewed simply as an industry or as an influence on government commercial policy, the Canadian industry is small compared with most of its Atlantic cousins. We have argued that, in a market context, it is a comparatively strong cousin, but this should not blind us to the fact that the entrenched position of the steel industries in the national policies of other countries might be too much to take on.

But a more favourable answer can be given to the second question—in regard to broad free trade arrangements embracing other products as well as steel. In the event of such free trade arrangements with some offshore Atlantic nations, Canadian steel has little to fear from any of the European producers—provided there is adherence to North American standards of competitive behaviour. Given the assumption of a general free trade arrangement between Canada and the EFTA, and perhaps also including the EEC, our main effort might successfully be directed towards retaining the industry we have developed and towards avoiding an extension of the conditions now existing in most of the European steel industries. Under the circumstances, much would depend upon the manner in which outstanding non-tariff problems would be negotiated in the over-all agreement.

This leaves us with the question of a Canadian-American free trade arrangement that included steel. For the steel industry, this idea starts with the advantages of common bonds of market practices and competitive behaviour, even though, by contrast with Canadian-American arrangements for other sectors, the meeting ground of common corporate interests is absent. There are also the existing flows of steel trade, though the role of the United States as a steel supplier to Canada has greatly diminished, while Canadian steel has made some headway in the regional U.S. markets that are within competitive reach of our production points. On the non-tariff commercial-policy side, a Canadian-American approach has the advantage of being free of many of the non-tariff obstacles present in our offshore analysis, though theoretically the Canadian general manufacturers' sales tax stands in the way of parallel treatment of each other's imports.[42]

[42]This, of course, is the result of structural differences in the two countries' tax systems. It is partly offset by the sales taxes of various states.

Viewed from the Canadian side, in terms of the range of products supplied by our industry, the elimination of the remaining North American steel tariffs would put no major Canadian consumption point in a position where it could be supplied from the United States competitively at existing price levels. For most products this extends even to the Canadian west coast, into which western U.S. producers face railroad freight costs similar to those of the Ontario plants. To the extent that the Canadian mills do not compete in every possible specification of various rolling mill products, U.S. mills, upon removal of the 10 percent Canadian steel tariff, would gain an advantage over offshore steel; but in the light of the present level of European export prices, this might be insufficient for an alteration in recent trade patterns.

With reference to steel, then, a Canadian-American free trade agreement would inherently enhance the market opportunities of the Canadian mills, to the extent that the elimination of the tariff would give them additional scope for absorbing freight costs. At a minimum, the Ontario steel mills would find their competitiveness at major U.S. midwestern steel-consumption points improved. Under existing base-price and exchange rate differentials, the same does not hold for the U.S. steel mills. However, given the present position of the U.S. steel industry, a Canadian-American arrangement limited to steel would be unlikely to attract support in the United States. Furthermore, a specific Canadian-American agreement in steel might face rough going at the GATT. In the foreseeable future the ripest area for Canadian-American cooperation limited to the steel sector would therefore most probably lie in jointly promoting international understanding and agreement on non-tariff commercial policies. Viewed somewhat differently, the American position regarding the steel sector by itself would certainly shy away from a specific Canadian commitment before it had settled its outstanding "problems" with the rest of the world.

At the same time, if our assessment is correct, the Canadian primary iron and steel industry can confidently approach the prospect of a more general Canada-U.S. free trade framework. This is on the assumption that such a generalized agreement would have definite arrangements for the maintenance and growth of the important steel-consuming industries, perhaps arrangements such as are part of the Canada-U.S. automotive products agreement, but in any event, as a minimum, a set of adequate transitional techniques. This study has, of course, not dealt with the economics of the major steel-consuming industries, though it can be concluded that, to the extent that an efficient and competitive source of steel supply is a determining factor, the Canadian steel industry would be a plus factor in maintaining and improving the position of steel-consuming industries in Canada.

All in all, with respect to a broad Canadian-American free trade framework, Canadian steel has become a key industry which can look forward with considerable confidence to the opportunities of a more integrated North American market.

Bibliography

Walter Adams and Joel B. Dirlam, "Big Steel, Invention and Innovation," *Quarterly Journal of Economics*, LXXX, no. 2, May 1966.

Algoma Steel Corporation, *Statistical Supplement to the Submission to the Minister of Finance* (Toronto, 1967).

Department of Energy, Mines and Resources, *Metallurgical Works in Canada, Primary Iron and Steel*, Operators List, Part 1, Ottawa, Jan. 1967.

Department of Energy, Mines and Resources, *Mineral Information Bulletin MR 70*, "The Canadian Steel Industry: A Pattern of Growth," Ottawa (no date).

Department of Trade and Commerce, "Agreement on Implementation of Article VI of the General Agreement on Tariffs and Trade" (mimeo.), Ottawa, 1967.

Department of Trade and Commerce, *Private and Public Investment in Canada*, Ottawa (annual).

Dominion Bureau of Statistics:

Aggregate Productivity Trends, 1946–1966, cat. no. 14–201, 1967.

Fixed Capital Flows and Stock, Manufacturing, Canada, 1926–1960, Methodology, cat. no. 13–522, February 1967.

Fixed Capital Flows and Stock, Manufacturing, Canada, 1926–1960, Statistical Supplement, cat. no. 13–523, August 1966.

Index of Industrial Production, cat. no. 61–005 (monthly).

Iron and Steel Mills, cat. no. 41–203 (annual).

Primary Iron and Steel, cat. no. 41–001 (monthly).

Productivity Trends in Industry, Report No. 1, cat. no. 14–502 (occasional), 1966.

Review of Man-Hours and Hourly Earnings, cat. nos. 72–002 and 72–202 (monthly and annual).

Revised Index of Industrial Production, 1935–1957, cat. no. 61–502, 1959.

Trade of Canada, Exports (monthly).

Trade of Canada, Imports (monthly).

William J. Hogan, s.j. "The Steel Import Problem: A Question of Quality and Price," *Thought*, XL, no. 159, New York, Winter 1965.

Japan Iron and Steel Federation, *Statistical Yearbook for 1965*, Tokyo, 1966.

C. P. Kindleberger, *Foreign Trade and the National Economy*, New Haven, Yale University Press, 1962.

Irving Kravis and others, "Measuring International Price Competitiveness: A Preliminary Report," National Bureau of Economic Research, *Occasional Paper 94*, New York, 1965.

Irving B. Kravis and Robert E. Lipsey, "The Measurement of Price Change: A Report on the Study of International Price Competitiveness," *American Economic Review, Papers and Proceedings*, LVII, no. 2, May 1967, pp. 482–91.

Francis Masson and J. B. Whitely, *Barriers to Trade between Canada and the United States*, Montreal and Washington, Canadian-American Committee, 1960.

National Bureau of Economic Research, *Foreign Tax Policies and Economic Growth*, a conference report of the National Bureau of Economic Research and the Brookings Institution, New York, 1966.

Organisation for Economic Co-operation and Development, Special Committee for Iron and Steel, *The Iron and Steel Industry* (annual issues), Paris.

Organisation for European Economic Co-operation, *The Iron and Steel Industry in Europe* (annual issues), Paris.

Royal Commission on Canada's Economic Prospects, *The Canadian Primary Iron and Steel Industry* (prepared by the Bank of Nova Scotia), Ottawa, October 1956.

Statistical Office of the European Communities, *Eisen und Stahl, 1966 Jahrbuch*, Brussels (no date).

Tariff Board, *Report . . . Respecting Basic Iron and Steel Products, Reference No. 118*, Ottawa, February 1957.

United Kingdom, Iron and Steel Board, *Development in the Iron and Steel Industry, Special Report 1964*, London, 1964.

United Nations, Economic Commission for Europe, *Automation in the Iron and Steel Industry*, New York, 1965.

United Nations, Economic Commission for Europe, *The European Steel Market* (annual issues), Geneva.

United Nations, Economic Commission for Europe, *Statistics of World Trade in Steel, 1913–1959*, Geneva, 1961.

United Nations, Economic Commission for Europe, *Statistics of World Trade in Steel* (annual issues), New York.

U.S. Senate, Committee on Finance, 90th Congress, 1st session, *Steel Import Study*, Washington, 1967.

U.S. Bureau of Labor Statistics, *Monthly Labour Review*, Washington (D.C.).

Jacob Viner, *Dumping: A Problem in International Trade*, Chicago, The University of Chicago Press, 1923.

J. H. Young, *Canadian Commercial Policy*, Royal Commission on Canada's Economic Prospects, Ottawa, 1957.

Newspapers:

American Metal Market (New York)

Metal Bulletin (London)

The Wall Street Journal (New York)

RELATED PUBLICATIONS BY THE
PRIVATE PLANNING ASSOCIATION OF CANADA

CANADIAN TRADE COMMITTEE PUBLICATIONS

THE WORLD ECONOMY

The World Economy at the Crossroads: A Survey of Current Problems of Money, Trade and Economic Development, by Harry G. Johnson, 1965.
The International Monetary System: Conflict and Reform, by Robert A. Mundell, 1965
International Commodity Agreements, by William E. Haviland, 1963.

CANADA'S TRADE RELATIONSHIPS

Canada's International Trade: An Analysis of Recent Trends and Patterns, by Bruce Wilkinson, 1968.
Canada's Trade with the Communist Countries of Eastern Europe, by Ian M. Drummond, 1966.
Canada's Role in Britain's Trade, by Edward M. Cape, 1965.
The Common Agricultural Policy of the E.E.C. and Its Implications for Canada's Exports, by Sol Sinclair, 1964.
Canada's Interest in the Trade Problems of Less-Developed Countries, by Grant L. Reuber, 1964.

CANADA'S COMMERCIAL POLICY AND COMPETITIVE POSITION

Prices, Productivity, and Canada's Competitive Position, by N. H. Lithwick, 1967.
Industrial Structure in Canada's International Competitive Position: A Study of the Factors Affecting Economies of Scale and Specialization in Canadian Manufacturing, by H. Edward English, 1964.
Canada's Approach to Trade Negotiations, by L. D. Wilgress, 1963.

CANADIAN-AMERICAN COMMITTEE PUBLICATIONS

CANADA-U.S. ECONOMIC RELATIONS

Constructive Alternatives to Proposals for U.S. Import Quotas (a Statement by the Committee), 1968.
U.S.-Canadian Free Trade: The Potential Impact on the Canadian Economy, by Paul Wonnacott and Ronald J. Wonnacott, 1968.
The Role of International Unionism in Canada, by John H. G. Crispo, 1967.
A New Trade Strategy for Canada and the United States (a Statement by the Committee), 1966.
Capital Flows between Canada and the United States, by Irving Brecher, 1965.
A Possible Plan for a Canada-U.S. Free Trade Area (a Staff Report), 1965.
Invisible Trade Barriers between Canada and the United States, by Francis' Masson and H. Edward English, 1963.
Non-Merchandise Transactions between Canada and the United States, by John W. Popkin, 1963.
Policies and Practices of United States Subsidiaries in Canada, by John Lindeman and Donald Armstrong, 1961.